General Editor's Preface

Contrasts in History is designed for use by students preparing for G.C.E. O Level and S.C.E. O Grade examinations. The volumes in the series could also be used for work of a more advanced nature.

Although the need to provide a narrative framework is not overlooked, the real intention is that each volume, by identifying and analysing problems, should introduce readers to the complexities of historical personalities and situations.

It is hoped that a series which illustrates the many-sided nature of events and periods, examines contrasts within and between societies, demonstrates the interplay of change and continuity, and seeks to create an awareness of differing interpretations, will help to build up a sense of the past and encourage the development of thinking skills.

DUNCAN MACINTYRE

Acknowledgments

The author and publisher wish to thank the following for permission to reproduce photographic material:

Punch: *pages 1, 31, 54, 67*
Fine Art Society: *page 2*
Illustrated London News: *pages 6, 45, 74*
The Mansell Collection: *pages 14, 23*
Radio Times Hulton Picture Library: *page 17 (two)*
Gladstone Library: *page 34*
Mrs Eva Reichmann and Captain Sir Thomas Barlow: *page 37*
Ulster Museum: *pages 43, 46*
Fawcett Library: *page 57*
Museum of London: *page 59*

Contents

1

A Golden Age?

The Edwardian period has often been viewed, in retrospect, by those who lived through it as a lost golden age: *... a time when life had a great deal of beauty and charm.*[1]

The nostalgic view of the Edwardian Age—straw boaters,
picture hats, a band playing on a hot, lazy day in midsummer.

Nostalgia is a constant flaw in the attitude of those looking back, and as one writer commented:

distance may lend enchantment to a view and time enhance the glories of a season.[2]

Memories tend to exaggerate the good things of life and conceal or overlook the bad; the older one grows the more the years that have passed become the "Good Old Days". It can be argued, however, that those who see the Edwardian era in this light can be excused, since the times that they describe fall between an economic depression at the end of the long Victorian age and the carnage of the First World War.

Charles Furth has confessed that:

Many of us, looking back, see the period before 1914 in the golden haze of a lost leisure, of a gracious and unhurried way of living. It seems always to have been a gentle summer. . . .[3]

"Death demanded the best and got it." This cartoon by Raemaekers aptly suggests the "dark chasm" of World War I, over which the memories of the Edwardian era have to leap.

The war of 1914–18 has been identified as one of the major elements determining the nature of these comments about the Edwardian era. Is it little wonder that the age was seen as golden for those looking back over the black wall of the First World War? J. B. Priestley's memoirs describe *"a time and a land seen across the vast chasm of war"*.[4]

However, to epitomize the Edwardian years as a golden age is to close one's eyes to the reality of its contrasting qualities. Behind the glamorous, glittering veneer that marked the style of high society lurked a mean, poverty-stricken "submerged" stratum. Behind the so-called political stability of the era lay serious constitutional questions posed by the People's Budget and the stance of the House of Lords, unrest in Ireland and of organized labour. Behind the romanticized image of the fashionable Edwardian lady were the wilful political ambitions of the Suffragette. Behind the apparent prosperity there was anxiety in the economy about industrial retardation and foreign competition. And behind the peace there were the storm clouds of war.

---

[1]Dame Irene Vanbrugh, quoted in *Scrapbook 1900–14* by L. Baily (MULLER, 1957); [2]Arthur Taylor, "The Economy" in *Edwardian England* by S. Nowell-Smith (ed.) (OXFORD, 1964); [3]*Life since 1900* by Charles Furth (ALLEN & UNWIN, 1956); [4]*The Edwardians* by J. B. Priestley (Heinemann, 1970)

2

Conspicuous Consumption

While it is difficult to ignore the effects of the First World War in creating a nostalgic impression of the Edwardian era, it should not be thought that this was the only reason for such an impression—it was indeed a golden age. Evidence for.this is found in the recollections of Mrs C. S. Peel published in 1933 under the title of *Life's Enchanted Cup*. The following extract describes aspects of upper middle class life in 1900 when her family were moving into a modernized house—complete with service lift, electric light and telephone—in Brompton Square, London:

> . . . [*it*] *contained a large basement, three sitting rooms, a lounge-hall, and seven bedrooms . . . all were warmed by coal fires . . . we entertained a good deal in a small way. Yet we found little difficulty in running the house with a staff consisting of a Norland nurse, a parlourmaid, a housemaid and a cook. Later we kept a manservant for £70 a year. The cook earned £28. The Norland nurse's salary was £40.*
>
> *Later, while our second child was in the nursery stage, we had a between maid. We spent about 12s. a head each week on food and cleaning materials, which included the cost of come-and-go guests, but not of parties. There was penny postage, no insurance to pay for domestic servants, stamps on cheques cost 1d. each and, most important of all, Income Tax was but 1s. in the £.*[1]

There is no sign here of anything but a comfortable and pleasant lifestyle and it is reinforced by study of the middle-class "budgets" which appeared in the *Cornhill Magazine* in 1901. A series of articles gave advice to readers on how to manage their incomes. For instance for someone earning £800 a year the advice was:

> . . . [*spend*] *at least £130 . . . on rent, rates and taxes . . . servants. Two is the right number, a cook at £20 a year, and house parlourmaid at £18 . . . [the husband] should be his own butler, and besides taking charge of the cellar, should decant, if not the everyday claret or whisky, certainly any wine which he offers to his friends. The wife should dust the china and*

ornaments; it prevents breakages, and gives the servant more time to get
through her morning's task of scrubbing, sweeping, silver cleaning,
and the like . . .
We now come to the sum necessary for housekeeping expenses . . . with
careful management [they] can be covered by £4 a week

	£	s.	d.
Washing (including household linen and servants' washing)		12	0
Window cleaning		1	4
Meat	1	0	0
Groceries	1	0	0
Bread		4	0
Vegetables		3	6
Milk		3	6
Eggs		2	6
Butter		4	6
Fish		4	0
Bacon		3	0
	£3	18	4[2]

The writer then went on to suggest that the husband who earned £800
a year should spend the following on drink, in each year:

		£	s.	d.
Whisky	*4½ dozen at 36s.*	8	2	0
Claret	*9 dozen at 15s.*	6	15	0
Port	*1½ dozen at 42s.*	3	3	0
Sherry	*1 dozen at 32s.*	1	12	0
Brandy	*2 bottles at 5s.*		10	0
		£20	2	0[2]

Some debatable advice, by our standards, is offered:

The husband needs more pocket money than the wife, and the wife needs
more clothes than the husband.[2]

and even more so:

As for smoking, a man who marries on £800 a year must like a pipe
or learn to like it. If he is but a moderate smoker, smokes tobacco at 6s. 6d.
a pound, and allows himself 100 cigars and 200 or 300 cigarettes in the
year, he will cover his expenses in this direction with £10.[2]

Other items in their cost of living are discussed: newspapers, tobacco,
club fees, doctor's and chemist's bills, fuel, holidays, theatre, etc.

Afternoon tea on the lawns at the Ranelagh Club, Barnes, London

By Edwardian standards this couple would be regarded as very comfortably off but, by no means rich. A sociologist would be inclined to place them in the upper middle class; this placing would be based on salary, their two servants, and their house—perhaps typically built on a smallish plot, with three floors, a nursery at the top, three bedrooms, bathroom, kitchen, scullery, drawing room, dining room and study.

Comfort rather than extravagance would mark their lifestyle. Simple pleasures like cycling, visits to the zoo, the sing-song round the piano, and walking in the park on a Sunday after church would be indulged in. Holidays might be at the seaside or in the Lake District with the servants included. The relationship with the servants would be friendly and the servants given quite a deal of responsibility, especially as regards the children. Visits to the theatre and music hall, and occasional dinner parties would enliven the daily routine.

In the same magazine Lady Agnew, writing in August 1901, gave advice on how to live on £10,000 a year, for, as she said, "*an ordinary well-favoured couple.*"[3]! She offered the following advice:

... content yourself with the medium-sized "mansion", either in London or the country—or both. One of moderate size in an accessible part of London would represent from £450 to £500 a year, its rates and taxes about £150 and the upkeep, painting and repairs, an average of £200 a year. A good London house of this sort of rental, and kept in good condition, can easily be let every season for £600 or £700.[3]

A typical menu for a day in such a household was described in a lady's magazine of 1904:

BREAKFAST
Baked Sardines
Kidney Omelet
Grilled Ham

LUNCHEON
Boiled Cod and Egg Sauce
Steak Fingers and Ribbon Potatoes
Brooklyn Pudding
Cheese

DINNER
Tomato Soup
Lobster Cutlets
Roast Ribs of Beef, Browned Potatoes
Beetroot and White Sauce
Woodcocks on Toast
Pineapple Pudding. Rice Cream .
Stilton Cheese
Dessert Oranges, Portugal Plums
Nuts, Madeleine Cakes[4]

Much would depend on the quality of the servants employed and how effectively they could budget for these "gargantuan" meals.

Next, Lady Agnew costed this lifestyle:

A fair average for the housekeeping books, if flowers and vegetables are provided by the country house, would be from £20 to £22 a week. The wages of twelve or fourteen servants would average between £350 and £400, and the upkeep of a London and a country house in linen, etc, would be close upon £200. There would then be £200 yearly for wine, £130 for coal, £70 for lighting, £130 for the butler's book which includes all telegrams, postage of letters and parcels, hampers, cabs, etc.; £70 indoor liveries; £150 stationery and little bills.[3]

With two houses, Lady Agnew's *"ordinary well-favoured"* couple had to justify their existence by spending time in each; this meant moving their household twice a year at a cost of £150. Three children were assumed: two boys and a girl, and Lady Agnew encouraged the couple to *"give them the best of everything."*[3] This meant education at Eton for the boys, and the girl, at home, to be instructed in household management and the graces expected of a lady of her class.

Lady Agnew then complained:

Public rates and taxes are the final twist of the torture screw, and they will grind out of you close upon £500. This would be taking the income tax at 8d. or 9d. in the pound.[3]

For such people life in the Edwardian era must have seemed particularly pleasant, especially when the prices of articles and food in the shops were in the following range:

Beef	8 to 10d. per lb
Mutton	8 to 9½d. per lb
Pork	8½ to 9½d. per lb
Tea	1s. 4d. to 1s. 6d. per lb
Sugar	2 to 2½d. per lb
Bacon	10 to 11d. per lb
Cheese	8 to 9d. per lb
Butter	1s. 3d. to 1s. 4d. per lb
Potatoes (7 lb)	3½ to 4½d.
Bread per 4 lb loaf	5½ to 6d.
Milk per quart	3½ to 4d.
Coal per cwt	1s. 0d. to 1s. 3d.

An income of this kind, taken together with such prices, makes a dinner, for twenty people, costing £60, well within the budget of the £10,000 a year couple. Arthur Ponsonby, in *The Camel and the Needle's Eye* written in 1910, gives the menu for such a dinner:

MENU

Cantaloup Glacé

Tortue Claire

Bisque Nantua

Truites Saumonées Michigan

Mousse de Jambon à L'Escurial

Selle d'Agneau Montefiore

Poularde Strasbourgeoise

Salade Indienne

Cailles Flanqués d'Ortolans

Asperges Verts   Sauce Mousseuse

Pêches Framboisines

Friandises

Fauchonettes Suisses

Hock, Claret, Port, Coffee, and Liqueurs[5]

A menu like this was not unusual at the homes of the Edwardian upper classes, especially when they had guests to entertain. Such facts led to the comment by J. B. Priestley, an Edwardian himself:

Not since Imperial Rome can there have been so many signposts to gluttony.[6]

Contemporary critics too, like C. F. G. Masterman, complained:

Thousands of pounds representing the toil of years in the cultivation of choice flowers or rare wines are dissipated for the gratification of a few guests at an evening party.[7]

For people in this income group, certainly upwards of £3000 per year, it was an *"age of conspicuous consumption."*[8]

Extravagance marked the lifestyle of the very rich, and their attention was fully occupied by the demands of the rather innocuously named "season".

To the average man the Season comprises courts, levées, state dinners and balls, Royal garden parties and a few other events of the hardy annual class, but in reality these are merely the cream of the Season's features. The balls, for example, include private and semi-private dances and the balls for countless charities. The list of dinners, again, comprises innumerable regimental banquets, Empire Day banquets, political dinners, Derby Day dinners, such as that at which the Duchess of Devonshire entertained Her Majesty and thirty other guests in 1907 and afterwards received a thousand favoured friends, county dinners, dinners in aid of charities, and private dinners without number. . . .

The opera, the theatres, and concerts, sales of work, musical receptions at Mansion House and elsewhere, picture shows, meetings in aid of charities, Congresses, lectures, May Meetings and Primrose League fixtures, exhibitions, the Horse Show, Military Tournament, cricket, croquet, lawn tennis, and other sporting events, bring together great crowds of people. The Henley Regatta, the Bisley meeting, Ascot, the Fourth of June at Eton, Speech Day at Harrow, Ballooning at Hurlingham and Ranelagh, and countless garden parties, are also important items . . . that assist to fully occupy the time of those who pursue the giddy round of pleasure.[9]

J. B. Priestley has argued that the *"giddy round of pleasure"* was tiring and that the epithet "the idle rich"—*"the byword of the moment"* according to Queen magazine—hardly applied:

Fashion and the social round . . . are ferocious taskmasters. To keep in, to keep going members of Edwardian high society toiled harder than overworked clerks or warehousemen.[6]

Recovery was aided by taking "a cure" in the autumn. Many of the self-indulgent rich went off annually to Austrian and

German spas—the most favoured were Marienbad, Baden-Baden, Ems, Homburg and Weisbaden. Winter holidays, too, became popular: the south of France, especially the resorts of Biarritz, Mentone, Nice, Cannes and Monte Carlo provided milder weather than Britain, and their gambling casinos daring entertainment. Winter sports attracted many to Switzerland. Such enterprises gave scope to critics:

> It [the upper class] has annexed whole regions abroad, Biarritz and the Riviera coast, Austrian and German watering places, whether it journeys for the recovery of its lost health, and for distractions which will forbid the pain of thinking.[10]

In Britain the great hotels of seaside and country opened their doors to the pleasure-seeking rich; golf was taken up avidly:

> Golf, of course, had long been a fashion but it was only now that not to play put one outside the pale.[11]

Lawn tennis too developed widely; and travel was easy and comfortable for the restless rich. "What is the life of the rich man today?" asked Lady Dorothy Nevill. "A sort of firework! Paris, Monte Carlo, big game shooting in Africa, fishing in Norway, dashes to Egypt, trips to Japan."[12]

The weekend house party epitomized the lifestyle of the rich. Off they went on a Friday to their country house, with mountains of luggage, to eat, drink, and take the air. No expense was spared; eating and drinking took up a great deal of their time:

> breakfast alone would make one of our Christmas dinners look meagre.[6]

A motor car excursion, hunting, riding or merely walking whiled away the daylight hours. Evening was for dinner, conversation, usually of a political kind, billiards, bridge or party games like charades. But the entertainment did not stop there:

> . . . the Edwardian house-party, while severely determined to keep up appearances, discreetly provided opportunities for lovers, not necessarily young, to enjoy themselves, the males having been fortified by a drink or two, a last ham sandwich or a bit of devilled chicken . . . many of these huge rambling mansions might have been designed for late-night sexual enterprise . . .[6]

Every Edwardian lady had to pay careful regard to fashion and dress etiquette, especially at a house party. Cynthia Asquith described the demands:

> You came down to breakfast in your best dress, usually made of velvet, and after church changed into tweeds. Another change for tea—into a tea-gown . . . a different dinner gown was considered essential for each evening. Thus a Friday to Monday party involved taking your "Sunday best", two tweed coats and skirts, three garments suitable for tea, your

"best hat"—a vast affair loaded with feathers, fruit or corn—a variety of
country head gear . . . numerous accessories in the way of petticoats, stoles,
scarves, evening wreaths . . . and a large bag in which to carry round the
house your embroidery.[13]

If you were very very rich or an aristocrat you might well be honoured by the presence of the King and Queen at your house party. But the Countess of Warwick sounded a note of caution:

The extravagance involved in country house entertaining was so considerable
that some of Royalty's friends could not afford it . . . I could tell stories of
men and women who had to economize for a whole year, or, alternatively,
get into debt, that they might entertain Royalty for one weekend![14]

King Edward VII was at the very top of this society; he set the pace by restoring the monarchy to London and *"lit up and flung open Buckingham Palace"*. He shared the tastes of this society and was thus quite unlike his mother, Queen Victoria. But his nephew, the German Kaiser, complained about the looseness in British high society and was angered by the report of an incident at a country house weekend attended by the German Crown Prince, where:

there had been unseemly romping in unlighted corridors, and one lady had
even gone so far as to take off her slipper.[15]

Many of the wealthy middle classes aped the extravagant ways of high society and were often difficult to distinguish from the real "high society" members. It is this frivolous tone of high society and the apparent self-indulgence of the upper middle class rich that has given rise to the popular view of the Edwardian age.

But the era was punctuated by comment critical of the gaiety and frivolity. *The Times* in 1913 saw the upper class rich indulging in *"a luxurious expenditure as fantastic as a veritable Dance of Death"*[16], while C. F. G. Masterman wrote:

At the one end of the scale the lives of a large proportion of the rich are
far from satisfactory. Separated from many of the realities of life, they are
unable to find natural ways of expending their money, and, in consequence,
are driven to indulge in sumptuous living, or in vulgar display.[7]

A golden age can only be founded on economic stability and prosperity; superficially the economy may have seemed sound to the self-indulgent rich, although we have the suggestion that even they saw the extravaganza coming to an end. As Priestley puts it:

There was a vague feeling that the end was almost in sight, that their class
was now banging away in the last act.[6]

His view could well be tinged with hindsight, but it is an echo of R. S. A. Palmer who suggested in 1911 that, *"The descent lies before us."*

Vera Brittain, by contrast, was perhaps more typical of the generation when she wrote in 1933 of:

> *That unparalleled age of rich materialism and tranquil comfort, which we who grew up at its close will never see again, appeared to us to have gone on from time immemorial, and to be securely destined to continue for ever.*[17]

Indeed most contemporaries believed that the economy was able to sustain the golden age; that, moreover, the Edwardian era had political and constitutional stability, peace and prosperity. But in fact this was a superficial view.

---

[1]*Life's Enchanted Cup* by C. S. Peel (BODLEY HEAD, 1933); [2] G. Colmore, *Cornhill Magazine*, June 1901, quoted in *Human Documents of the Age of the Forsytes* by E. Royston Pike (ed.) (ALLEN & UNWIN, 1969); [3]Lady Agnew, *Cornhill Magazine*, August 1901, quoted in Royston Pike *op cit.*; [4]*The Lady's Realm* (ARROW, 1972); [5]*The Camel and the Needle's Eye* by A. Ponsonby (FIFIELD, 1910); [6]J. B. Priestley *op cit.*; [7]*The Heart of the Empire* by C. F. G. Masterman (rep. HARVESTER, 1901); [8]*Theory of the Leisure Class* by T. Veblen (1899); [9]H. Macfarland, "£ s d of a London Season" in *The Lady's Realm* (1909); [10]*The Condition of England* by C. F. G. Masterman (METHUEN, 1909); [11]*Punch*, 19 July 1911; [12]*Reminiscences* by Lady Dorothy Nevill (1906); [13]*The Day Before Yesterday* by Cynthia Asquith (COLLINS, 1956); [14]*Afterthoughts* by Countess of Warwick (CASSELL, 1931); [15]*Lord Lansdowne* by Lord Newton (MACMILLAN, 1929); [16]*The Times*, 1 January 1913; [17]*Testament of Youth* by Vera Brittain (COLLANCZ, 1933)

3

Dark Shadows

I n glaring contrast to the outward prosperity and gaiety of the Edwardian golden age was the persistent degrading misery of vast numbers of people.

Mrs Peel, and others like her, portrayed *their* segment of society: the upper middle class and aristocracy. But at most they composed only about five per cent of the population. Eighty per cent made up the working class: mostly the wage earners in industries, but including small shopkeepers, hawkers, dressmakers and perhaps also about another half a million men and women who earned less than £160 a year. Everyone else, i.e. some fifteen per cent, made up the middle class; here one would find doctors, lawyers, clergymen, engineers, artists, writers, entertainers, law clerks, teachers, farmers, and provincial businessmen.

It was inside the eighty per cent that the poor were found. It would be easy to generalize and say that all the eighty per cent were poor. Indeed that was, more or less, how Leo Chiozza Money, a Liberal M.P. and comfortably-off himself, viewed Edwardian society in his book, *Riches and Poverty*. It became an immediate bestseller and went into ten editions between 1904 and 1911. He attacked the rigid class distinctions and vast inequalities of the time.

While we have acquired enormous wealth [as a people] and enjoy a magnificent national income, that wealth and that income are not so distributed as to give a sufficiency of material things to all our population . . . Contrasts between great riches and extreme poverty are everyday presented to our eyes . . . Those persons who have more than £160 per annum enjoy an aggregate income of £830,000,000. Those persons who have less than £160 per annum enjoy an aggregate income of £880,000,000.[1]

Chiozza Money then estimated how many people had an income of £160 and upwards and subdivided them into "rich" and "comfortable". Those with less than £160 he labelled the "poor". This allowed him to draw the following diagram:

RICH	COMFORTABLE
1,250,000 persons	*3,750,000 persons*
£585,000,000	£245,000,000

POOR

38,000,000 persons

£880,000,000

But, by modern standards, Chiozza Money was using inadequate data rather crudely to punctuate his contention about the fundamental inequalities of income distribution in the Edwardian era. One would hesitate to reject his general thesis, but modern social historians, by applying more sophisticated techniques of analysis, have come up with a rather more accurate picture of Edwardian society, though one which does not remove the glaring contrast between top and bottom.

Waiting for the next race at Ascot in 1904

Societies are never absolutely static, and there had been in the last quarter of the 19th century a significant rise in the real earnings of the working classes—in some exceptional cases as high as forty per cent. This meant that gradations had appeared within the rungs of the social ladder and had sometimes blurred the lines of class division.

From the middle of the 1890s the increase in real wages, i.e. what money from the pay packet will actually buy, began to slow down because of the rising prices of imports and reduced productivity at home. When the Edwardian era dawned, it seemed that working-class incomes had become almost stationary. These trends are indicated clearly here:

Relationship between Prices and Nominal and Real Wages

Period	Nominal Wages (Pay packet amount)	Prices	Real Wages (What money will actually buy)
1870—73	Rising very fast	Rising fast	Rising fast
1873—79	Falling fast	Falling fast	Nearly static
1879—87	Nearly static	Falling	Rising
1887—92	Rising	Rising/Falling	Rising
1892—97	Nearly static	Falling	Rising
1897—1900	Rising fast	Rising	Rising
1900—1914	Stationary	Rising	Falling slowly

Thus in real terms, wages fell slightly during the period 1900–14. Even more galling to the workers, at least, was that the "conspicuous consumption" that marked the lifestyle of the rich and the upper middle class, seemed to suggest that the rich were actually becoming richer: a phenomenon often commented on in the Press especially in relation to the number of motor cars on the roads. More likely the increasing number of cars was an indication that the wealthy were spending money on cars rather than on other things. But to many, motor cars were *"visible symbols of the selfishness of arrogant wealth."*[2]

Income tax figures for the period show that the total number of taxpayers was growing, but not the total average sum declared. Obviously within the tax-paying group there was scope for variation; indeed some individuals reaped large returns from investments overseas at this time. Generally, however, while it might be true that the rich in total did not have more to spend, it seemed, if the London season was any gauge to go by, that more was being spent, or seen to be spent by more people. Even if the gap between rich and poor had not in effect widened, it still yawned dangerously.

The existence of this gap was not a new fact for Edwardians. As early as 1883 there had been published anonymously a penny pamphlet which described the full horror of life in the slums of Bermondsey in London. Its title was *The Bitter Cry of Outcast London*. In twenty unvarnished pages its author, Rev. Andrew Mearns, in charge of a non-conformist mission, exposed the problem of abject poverty. Almost immediately it created a public conscience on the slum problem; its tone was uncompromising:

> *Every room in these rotten and reeking tenements houses a family, often two. In one cellar . . . a father, mother, three children and four pigs! In another room a man ill with smallpox, his wife just recovering from her eighth confinement, and the children running about half naked and covered with dirt . . . seven people living in one underground kitchen and a little dead child lying in the same room. . . .*
>
> *That people condemned to exist under such conditions take to drink and fall into sin is surely a matter for little surprise. . . .*
>
> *Who can wonder that every evil flourishes in such hotbeds of vice and disease? Who can wonder that little children taken from these hovels to the hospital cry, when they are well, through dread of being sent back to their former misery? Who can wonder that young girls wander off into a life of immorality, which promises release from such conditions? Who can wonder that the public house is "the Elysian-field of the tired toiler"?*[3]

A spate of articles, pamphlets and books followed on Mearns. The Churches declared their concern and leading public figures debated what was to be done. Despite the growing public awareness of the problem, the somewhat Victorian belief that slum families mostly chose to live where they did and squander their money on drink or gambling rather than spend it wisely on their homes, lived on.

Human vice and weakness were said to be the prime cause of slum conditions. Indeed some people thought that slums were almost "immortal" and could never be eradicated; others suggested that if baths were provided the slum dwellers would store coal in them!

By the beginning of the Edwardian era the problem had not receded at all; nor were there many significant improvements initiated by government or local authorities—cost was a major obstacle, particularly to housing improvement. In the case, for instance, of the London County Council's first slum clearance scheme in Bethnal Green between 1890 and 1900, where demolition costs alone worked out at about £300 per family, the better housing had attracted a higher social grade to move in, thus displacing the poorer original inhabitants who added to the overcrowding elsewhere.

Children of "the haves" with their nanny in London's Hyde Park, 1911

Children of "the have-nots" with their parents in London's East End

A greater concern was shown on the publication of the work of pioneer sociologists like Charles Booth (1840–1916), the successful and rich shipping merchant, and Seebohm Rowntree (1871–1954), the Quaker, philanthropist, cocoa manufacturer. Unlike Mearns and the others previously, Booth and Rowntree both set out to study the poverty problem systematically and to produce statistical data on their areas.

Booth's was a mammoth survey, begun in 1889 and not completed until 1903. It ran to seventeen volumes and was entitled *The Life and Labour of the People of London*. Initially he focused attention solely on the East End but later widened it to include all London to check how far the poverty he discovered in the East End was repeated throughout the metropolis.

As far as the East End was concerned he came to the following conclusions:

1. The poor made up nearly thirty-five per cent of the 900,000 living in East London.
2. 185,000 belonged to families earning less than 18 shillings a week.
3. Over 100,000 suffered from acute "distress".

From the East End, Booth extended his study to include the rest of London. This was a more superficial study than the depth with which he had looked at the East End, but he was surprised to find that even in the rest of London pockets of poverty existed almost as had as in the East End. Indeed he calculated that 30.7 per cent of London's entire population were in poverty and that often the poor lived in the same districts as the middle and upper classes, their lifestyles presenting obvious contrasts.

Admittedly Booth's work lacked "precision", although it was in advance of Mearns's study. Its conclusion was startling enough: thirty per cent poverty in a society experiencing a golden age! Perhaps even more significant than the actual poverty level, was Booth's quite astonishing analysis of its causes. Of those living in poverty, about two-thirds were in that position because of low pay or irregular earnings, about one quarter because of illness or infirmity, and only about one-tenth because of personal failings such as drunkenness, laziness or thriftlessness. Booth's evidence demolished the myth often perpetrated by the middle class that poverty resulted from personal failure, vice or bad budgeting.

Rowntree, by contrast, was much more systematic and confined his study to York, his home city, the problems of which he knew well. It was small enough, with its 15,000 houses and population of

75,812, to make possible a visit to every working-class home. In fact 11,560 families were studied, amounting to 46,754 people.

The comparative smallness of the population in York enabled the enquiry to be carried out with an amount of detail that was impossible in London.[4]

He argued, also, that if a historic and well-known city like York had deep-rooted poverty, it would be an impressive demonstration of the extent of Britain's social problem. Investigations of industrial giants like Glasgow, Birmingham and Manchester were almost bound to find poverty traps, but if York had them too . . . ?

Information was obtained over a period of seven months— remarkable for its time—by a chief paid investigator with help from a part-time team of investigators. In most cases, housewives answered the questions posed on the state of the houses, the size of the rent, the age of the householders, the number of wage earners. Each investigator added a brief comment of his own such as "clean and respectable", "tidy" or "untidy", "dirty", "overcrowded". The whole enterprise was published in 1901 as *Poverty, a Study of Town Life.* Rowntree had no political axe to grind; only his conscience was stirred:

I did not set out upon my inquiry with the object of proving any pre-conceived theory, but to ascertain actual facts . . .[4]

This indeed he did! Here are a few striking examples:

Chimney sweep. Married. Two rooms. Five children under thirteen. All sleep in one room, wife just confined. Man in temporary employment, earning 2 shillings per day. House not very dirty. Man brought up in Industrial School, and is incapable of supporting his family decently. A bad workman. The house shares one closet with two other houses, and one water tap with three others. Rent 2s. 9d.[4]

Charwoman. Two rooms. Son (20 years) Casual labourer. Husband in workhouse. Dirt and drink in plenty. This house shares one water tap with six other houses, and one closet with two others. Rent 2s.[4]

Bricklayer's labourer. Married. Two rooms. Three children, school age or under. The stench here is abominable. The grating of the street drain is $1\frac{1}{2}$ yards from the house door and is blocked up. There are twenty-three houses in this yard, and only one water tap for the whole number. There is one ashpit from this yard: it is full to the top, and slime running down from the walls. Rent 2s. 3d.[4] [*He earned between 18s. and 21s. per week.*]

Tobacconist. Married. Two rooms. Good business. House consists of shop and kitchen. Twenty-one houses share one water tap and seven houses one closet. Rent 2s. 2d.[4] [*He earned over 30s. per week.*]

It is noticeable in the last case that a higher income did not necessarily ensure better housing.

But what conclusion did Rowntree reach about poverty in York?

Families regarded as living in poverty were grouped under two heads:

(a) Families whose total earnings were insufficient to obtain the minimum necessaries for the maintenance of merely physical efficiency. Poverty falling under this head was described as "Primary Poverty".

(b) Families whose actual total earnings would have been sufficient for the maintenance of merely physical efficiency were it not that some portion of it was absorbed by other expenditure, either useful or wasteful. Poverty falling under this head was described as "Secondary Poverty".

To ascertain the total number living in "Primary" poverty it was necessary to ascertain the minimum cost upon which families of various sizes could be maintained in a state of physical efficiency. This question was discussed under three heads, viz., the necessary expenditure for (1) Food; (2) Rent; and (3) All else. . . . for a family of father, mother and three children, the minimum weekly expenditure upon which physical efficiency can be maintained in York is 21s. 8d. made up as follows:

Food	12s.	9d.
Rent	4s.	0d.
Clothing, light, fuel, etc.	4s.	11d.
	21s.	8d.

The necessary expenditure for families larger or smaller than the above will be correspondingly greater or less. This estimate was based upon the assumptions that the diet is selected with . . . regard to the nutritive values of the various food stuffs, and that these are all purchased at the lowest current prices. It only allows for a diet less generous as regards variety than that supplied to able-bodied paupers in workhouses. It further assumes that no clothing is purchased which is not absolutely necessary for health, and assumes too that it is of the plainest and most economical description. No expenditure of any kind is allowed for beyond that which is absolutely necessary for the maintenance of merely physical efficiency. And let us clearly understand what "merely physical efficiency" means. A family living upon the scale allowed for in this estimate must never spend a penny on railway or omnibus; never go into the country unless they walk; never purchase a halfpenny newspaper or buy a ticket for a popular concert; never write letters to absent children, for they cannot afford the postage. They cannot save, join sick club or trade union; they cannot pay the sub-

scription. The children have no pocket money for dolls, marbles or sweets.
The father must not smoke or drink. The mother must never buy any
pretty clothes for herself or for her children. . . . Finally, the wage earner
must never be absent from his work for a single day. If any of these con-
ditions are broken, the extra income is met, and can only be met, by limiting
the diet; or in other words by sacrificing physical efficiency.

The number of persons whose earnings are so low that they cannot meet
the expenditure necessary for the above standard of living, . . . was . . .
7230, or almost exactly 10 per cent of the total population of the city. These
persons then, represent those who are in "primary poverty". The number
of those in "secondary poverty"; . . . 13,072, or 17.9 per cent of the total
population. In this way, 20,302 persons, or 27.84 per cent of the total
population were returned as living in poverty.

That in this land of abounding wealth, probably more than one fourth
of the population are living in poverty, is a fact which may well cause
great searchings of the heart. There is surely need for a greater concentra-
tion of thought by the nation upon the well-being of its own people, for no
civilisation can be sound or stable which has as its base this mass of stunted
human life.[4]

While the York inquiry was more comprehensive, it had reached much
the same conclusion as Booth in London.

As if these studies were not enough, many other Edwardians
pursued the spectre of poverty from various angles, and published
an immense mass of material. The afore-mentioned Chiozza Money
analysed the inequalities of Edwardian society:

Deprivation for the many and luxury for the few have degraded our
national life at both ends of the scale. At one end, "thirteen millions on
the verge of hunger", physically and morally deteriorated through poverty
and unloveliness. At the other, the inheritors of the earth, "senseless
conduits through which the strength and riches of their native land are
poured into the cup of the fornication of its capital".[1]

and more simply,

the United Kingdom is seen to contain a great multitude of poor people,
veneered with a thin layer of the comfortable and rich.[1]

In 1907 Lady Florence Bell wrote her study of Middlesbrough, a
typical industrial town with its *"furnaces, the grey streets, a few public*
buildings, all set in a background of greyness in a devastated landscape, under a
grey sky."[5] She, the wife of a prosperous ironmaster, described *"a*
struggling striving population of workmen and their families"[5] and the
"continuous toil" that was their life. At times she echoed the sentiments
of Rowntree when describing just how easily the worker by accident,

illness or unemployment could plunge into poverty from which it was not easy to recover:

> the path the iron worker daily treads at the edge of the sandy platform, that narrow path that lies between running streams of fire on the one hand and a sheer drop on the other is but an emblem of the road of life along which he must walk. If he should stumble either actually or metaphorically as he goes he has but a small margin in which to recover himself.[5]

She investigated 900 working-class households, and classified 125 as being *"absolutely poor"* and a further 175 as *"So near the poverty line that they are constantly passing over it."*[5] Other studies pointed out the same message: poverty in Britain was actual; a matter of facts and figures; a matter for public and political concern and, above all, action.

If we seek additional evidence we find it in *Poverty,* by Will Reason (1909); *The Minority Report of the Poor Law Commission* by Sidney and Beatrice Webb (1909); *The Living Wage* by Philip Snowden (1912); and in 1912 also a more academic approach was made by Professor Arthur Bowley of the London School of Economics in poverty surveys on a "sample" basis in five other provincial towns—Reading, Warrington, Northampton, Bolton and Hanley. The conclusions reached more or less substantiated Rowntree's: thirty-two per cent of the adult wage earners received less than 24 shillings per week and sixteen per cent of the working class was living in primary poverty.

Then there was the eloquent and influential work of C. F. G. Masterman—two books are worthy of mention: *The Heart of the Empire* (1901) and more important, *The Condition of England* (1909). No other contemporary social observer quite achieved the stylish prose of Masterman. Rowntree had described the poor and left out the rich: to Masterman the era presented a dominating contrast between rich and poor:

> We have converted half of the Highlands into deer forests for our sport, and the amount annually spent on shooting, racing, golf, on apparatus and train journeys and service, exceeds the total revenue of many a European principality. We fling away in ugly white hotels, in uninspired dramatic entertainments and in elaborate banquets, of which everyone is weary, the price of many poor men's yearly income.[6]

Edwardian Britain had become decadent:

> a society fissured into an unnatural plentitude *on the one hand* [*and*] as *its inevitable consummation a society fissured into* an unnatural privation *on the other.*[6]

Was this the "price of Prosperity"? asked Masterman.

WAITING TO BUY "TRIM-
MINGS" OF MEAT.

Government set up large-scale enquiries and reports were published; of these, the most important were *Earnings and Hours of Work* and *The Cost of Living of the Working Classes*; both provided data which could be related directly to Rowntree's standard physical efficiency wage of 21s. 8d. a week. It was shown that the average agricultural labourer was paid only 20s. per week, the jute worker 21s. 7d., the public utilities worker 28s. 1d., the engineer 32s. 5d. and the shipbuilder 35s. 1d.

Basing his ideas on the nutritional value of food, Rowntree had estimated that enough food to keep a man "physically efficient" could be bought for 3s. 3d. a week, a woman 2s. 9d. and children between 2s. 1d. and 2s. 7d. Few families in the lower classes had the ability to spend wisely enough to meet such standards, especially on account of rent, fuel and clothing commitments. Thus underfeeding was a normal aspect of Edwardian working-class life. At best, in many families, only one good meal was eaten a day and great reliance was placed on the regular sale of left-overs: broken eggs, pieces of meat, stale bread, bruised fruit, broken biscuits. One poor woman explained that in emergency the family pet rabbits could be eaten:

And the last one, it was a big white one, Billy we used to call it, beautiful thing. And my mother had no dinner one Sunday and he [father] killed this rabbit. And my mother couldn't eat it. She said, "I'm not eating my Billy". And my Dad was near to tears eating it . . . we never starved . . . my mother went without herself for us, yes. I've known her to wipe the plate round with a drop of gravy, and tell my father she'd had her dinner, she'd never had any.[7]

No amount of governmental data can illustrate more cogently the food problem of the poor. Between two thirds and three quarters of an ordinary working man's wage went on food. With wages so low no wonder there was widespread malnutrition in the industrial areas. A Glasgow Corporation Report of 1912 suggested that families earning less than £1 a week could not hope to have a satisfactory diet.

Throughout the era the rent of working-class houses remained quite stable: 1 shilling to 1s. 6d. for a small one-roomed cottage; 2s. 6d. for a large one-roomed house; 2s. 6d. to 3s. 6d. for a two-roomed house. But with nominal wages almost static and falling in real terms there was little chance that workers could improve their housing conditions. And where housing was improved by local authorities, it usually cost more than the poorest workers could afford. For instance, the rents for the City Improvement Trust Houses in Glasgow in 1906 were:

£5   for 1 apartment per annum (the single end)
£8   for 2 apartments per annum (the room and kitchen)
£12–13 for 3 apartments per annum

There exists plenty of evidence of the housing conditions of the lower classes in the Edwardian age: The Royal Commission on the Poor Law (1909), the Report on Housing and Industrial Conditions in Dundee (1905) and the 1911 Census are but three.

Birmingham had the unhealthiest housing of any large English city in 1914: 40,000 back-to-back houses, over 40,000 without any drainage or water tap, and nearly 60,000 without a separate W.C. London had the worst overcrowding in England: one sixth of its population was living with more than two people to a room (the Registrar General's definition of overcrowding).

Overall Scotland was even worse: about half the houses had only one or two rooms. The industrial belt showed up badly. In the mining town of Armadale (Midlothian) 83 per cent of the population lived in one or two rooms; it was more than 70 per cent in Airdrie, Clydebank, Lochgelly and Motherwell. Aberdeen was 38.6 per cent, Edinburgh 37 per cent and Perth 30 per cent. Glasgow was the most overcrowded city in the United Kingdom. Blocks of flats, called tenements, were common. In these the "room and kitchen" and the "single end" predominated; cooking, eating, washing and drying of clothes, and sleeping took place in the same rooms. There was little privacy.

Glasgow contrasted very unfavourably with the towns of southern England where the majority of houses had six or more rooms as well as a scullery, running water, gas, and often a bathroom; indeed in the south the old slum areas were small. But the towns of the industrial north of England, while not as bad as Glasgow, left much to be desired on health grounds with their back-to-back terraced dwellings of four or five rooms as typical. More than a quarter had no drainage and excrement had to be shovelled out of the privies at intervals by sanitary gangs into barrows and then emptied into carts in the street.

Governmental reports and the private surveys remain major sources for our knowledge of the working life of the Edwardian lower orders. But to obtain a closer insight and understanding of what it was like, individually, to be poor at this time, autobiographies are valuable. They tend to be honest and authentic, but sometimes the record's accuracy is clouded by personal or political motivation. This is very often so when the autobiographies of well-known people who moved from humble origins in the Edwardian period to positions of honour and respectability through hard work, self-education, thrift, concern for others, luck, etc. are used. Consider, for example, such disparate careers as Herbert Morrison[8] and Charlie Chaplin.[9]

The problem of ensuring accuracy is lessened if we take an ordinary person's record—though, of course, writing such a record does set even the ordinary somewhat apart from contemporaries. A good sociological "sample" of the Edwardian lower orders is Lilian Westall, born at Mortlake in 1893, one of nine children whose father, a maker of cricket bats, seems to have spent most of his wages on drink. These extracts are from her unpublished autobiography which she called *The Good Old Days*:

> *there were many times when most of his money had gone by Saturday night, and on the Monday the bedclothes, the blankets, my mother's wedding ring would all go in pawn to give us enough money to get through the week.*[10]

Lilian went to elementary school until she was 14 and she described her life up to that time:

> *In 1905 we lived in a terraced house in King's Cross with eight children under the age of fourteen in the family. There were three rooms, the main bedroom, another just big enough to take a double bed, and the front room which was bedroom, living room, kitchen. It held a bed, sofa, table, half a dozen chairs, a wash stand, an open grate on which my mother cooked all the meals, on fuel of wood-shavings, cinders and a little coal. Two other families lived in the same house; water had to be fetched from the wash-house in the yard; we shared the same outside lavatory.*

Six of us slept in one bed, three at the top, three at the bottom. . . .
Every morning I had to be down at the butcher's by seven o'clock . . . to
queue for "Threepenn'orth of pieces", the odds and ends from the trimmed
meat, about two pounds altogether, which were made into a stew with a
pennyworth of pot herbs as a dinner for all of us. At times there wasn't
enough food . . . and some of us would go down to the Salvation Army
hostel in Pentonville Road and get breakfast for a farthing; a cup of tea
and a large slice of bread and jam. At home, our tea was usually three
slices of bread and margarine each . . . Occasionally we would have a
ha'p'orth of syrup between us, or twopennyworth of speckled fruit, half-
rotten apples and soggy oranges.[10]

But Lilian was one of the fortunate. Others in the working
classes had to put up with much worse lives. Sub-human conditions
were the products of poverty and they had horrible side effects. The
first ten years of the century had the highest murder rate of any decade
before 1970. Prostitution claimed thousands of working-class girls
and plagued the major cities. Drunkenness was common. Above all,
it was the health of the working people that jolted the leading politicians to act on the problems, so keenly and expertly reported.

It was well known that the lack of sanitary facilities in the
slums of the cities led to rife enteric fever and diarrhoea, a major cause
of infant mortality. However, it was an article in the *Contemporary
Review* of January 1902 by Major General Sir John Frederick Maurice
that set the country, and especially the politicians, alight. Writing under
the pseudonym of "Miles", Maurice suggested the terrifying prospect
of national physical deterioration. He based his view on information
from recruiting for the army. Another article followed a year later. In
addition the figures, contained in a special report by the Director-
General, Army Medical Corps in 1903, of 34.6 per cent rejected as
medically unfit, coupled with the Interdepartmental Committee on
Physical Deterioration's findings made it clear just how drastic the
problem was. Britain had moved well away from the Balfour thinking
of 1900 that,

the time is not propitious for any dramatic reforms which involve a large
expenditure.

And the mood was now expressed by Prime Minister Campbell-
Bannerman:

England must be less of a pleasure ground for the rich and more of a
treasure house for the nation.

The veneer of the golden age wears thin when the social condition of
the mass of the population is considered.

[1]*Riches and Poverty* by L. Chiozza Money (METHUEN, 1905); [2]*England 1870-1914* by R. C. K. Ensor (OXFORD, 1936); [3]*The Bitter Cry of Outcast London* by A. Mearns (1883); [4]*Poverty, a Study of Town Life* by S. Rowntree (NELSON, 1901); [5]*At the Works* by F. Bell (NELSON, 1907); [6]*The Heart of the Empire* by C. F. G. Masterman *op. cit.*; [7]*The Edwardians* by P. Thompson (WEIDENFELD & NICOLSON, 1975); [8]*An Autobiography* by H. Morrison (ODHAMS, 1960); [9]*My Autobiography* by C. Chaplin (BODLEY HEAD, 1964); [10]quoted in *Useful Toil* by J. Burnett (ALLEN LANE, 1974)

4

Rebellious Peers

At the opening of Parliament on 21 February, 1910, King Edward VII, in his speech from the Throne, announced that measures would be introduced to:

define the relations between the Houses of Parliament, so as to secure the undivided authority of the House of Commons over finance and its predominance in legislation.

Behind the carefully chosen parliamentary language lurked a very critical issue which had come to dominate party politics in the Edwardian era: the role of the House of Lords in the making of legislation. Mirrored in the question, too, was the growing awareness and stark reality of the contrast between rich and poor in these times. Distance from the events has tended to tone down the tension of the struggle between the two Houses and allowed yet again the elegance and glitter of the age to blur our picture of the real political scene.

The issue was not a new one. When the Conservatives (then known as Unionists) had been in power from 1886 to December, 1905, with one interval of Liberal government from 1892 to 1895, they had little difficulty in pushing their legislative programme through both Commons and Lords. Events foreshadowing what was to come in the Edwardian era occurred in that short period of Liberal government. In 1893 the Lords mangled Gladstone's last attempt at Home Rule for Ireland by 419 to 41 votes, and went on to mutilate, usually by amendments, other progressive measures. The Liberals' leader, Lord Rosebery, complained to Queen Victoria:

When the Conservative Party is in power, there is practically no House of Lords . . . but the moment a Liberal Government is formed this harmless body assumes an active life, and its activity is entirely exercised in opposition to the Government. It is, in fact, a permanent barrier against the Liberal party.

The House of Lords did not regard itself as a kind of political backwater: it still possessed the right to veto, the right to throw out bills which had passed through the House of Commons. This was what Rosebery had experienced! The Queen retorted that Rosebery's grumble was *"a most revolutionary proceeding."* At that time the Liberals were reluctant to try to reduce the power of the Lords. The Conservatives were back in office in 1895.

By the accession of King Edward VII, the Conservative government had won yet another period of office and had come under the leadership of A. J. Balfour in 1902. Again they found no difficulty with the House of Lords. Some major legislation was passed: an Education Act in 1902, an Irish Land Purchase Act in 1903, and a Licensing Act in 1904. But even more significant achievements came from this government in relation to Britain's place in world affairs. A treaty was signed with Japan in 1902, and the Entente Cordiale was reached with France two years later; in the same year the Committee of Imperial Defence was set up—it was to become immensely important ten years later, and has been regarded as a *"far-seeing initiative"*.[1] Throughout this period again *"there* [was] *practically no House of Lords"*. But it was not all plain sailing. By December 1905 Balfour had steered his government into the doldrums of Chinese slavery, and, above all, tariff reform. He was forced to resign and the Liberals took office under Campbell-Bannerman. Parliament was promptly dissolved.

The election that followed swept the Liberals back in a landslide. The composition of the Commons was as follows:

Liberals	377 seats
Lib-Labs	24
Irish	83
Labour	29
Conservatives	132
Lib-Unionists	25

Labour and Irish M.Ps often voted with the government, and the Liberals could count on a majority of 356. Even if other parties combined against them, the Liberals and Lib-Labs had a majority of 132.

Few Conservatives realized just how disenchanted the electorate had become after a generation of Conservative governments. The new Prime Minister, Campbell-Bannerman, promised little in the way of specific proposals, but mentioned vaguely the need to make Britain *"less of a pleasure ground for the rich and more of a treasure house for the nation."* It was left to Asquith and others to strike home the Liberal programme for education, drink, trade union reform and old age pensions—what Balfour attacked as a *"long catalogue of revolutionary change"*.

But the electorate did not vote the Liberals in on the strength of their programme: much of it was still under discussion in the party and almost every leading Liberal had a different view. Liberal unity lay in their opposition to the bungling ineffectiveness of the Conservatives under Balfour. The victory of 1906 tended to be a negative one. However, with such a huge majority the Liberals ought to have found it easy to push through any legislative programme. Indeed, in at least one person's view:

> the outstanding feature of politics from 1903 to 1914 was . . . the absolute superiority of the Liberal party.[2]

Faced with this, what could the Conservatives effectively do? The question was all the more important since by then the Conservatives had grown so accustomed to being in power that they saw themselves almost with a natural right to govern. Indeed Balfour was exceedingly reluctant to admit defeat and had maintained, in a speech delivered at Nottingham on 15 January, 1906, that:

> the great Unionist Party should still control, whether in power or whether in opposition, the destinies of this Empire.

Few saw this as an attack on the democratic process or the constitution. But for Balfour it was more than a morale-boosting exercise for his Party. He meant what he said, and he would not be too choosy about the weapons used to achieve what he said. Tactics became essential to his own and his Party's political survival. He chose, as had been done in 1894, to exploit the position of the House of Lords in the making of Parliamentary legislation. On 13 April, 1906 he wrote to the Conservative leader in the Lords, Lansdowne:

> the two Houses shall not work as two separate armies but shall co-operate in a common plan of campaign.

In other words, the Lords would be used as the Conservatives' major weapon against the "revolutionary legislation" proposed by the Liberal Government. The case was stated bluntly by Balfour during debate on the 1906 Education Bill:

> The real discussion of this question is not now in this House . . . the real discussion must be elsewhere.

So real was that discussion that the Lords threw out the Education Bill.

From 1906 to 1908 Conservative tactics seemed to pay off. The Lords, more or less, controlled the passage of Liberal legislation and they did it skilfully. They were careful to accept the Trades Disputes Bill which overturned the contentious Taff Vale decision of 1902. But then they threw out the Education measure, the Plural Voting Bill, and a Licensing Bill. The Government itself withdrew an

THE NEW GUY FAWKES PLOT;
OR, THE BEST ADVERTISED CONSPIRACY IN THE WORLD.
[The First Autumn Meeting of the Cabinet has been summoned for the Fifth of November, Guy Fawkes Day.]

As early as October 1907 *Punch* showed that the Liberals, led by Campbell-Bannerman, intended to blow up the stubborn Lords, with measures pushed by Lloyd George.

Irish Devolution measure. In effect the Liberals did little in these years to justify their very large majority and their own high hopes. They were fully aware of what Balfour was doing and their frustration and anxiety drove the Prime Minister in December 1906 to set up a small Cabinet Committee to investigate the question of the reform of the Lords. Little however came of it. Instead Campbell-Bannerman opted for a three-day debate the following June on a resolution that "the will of the Commons must prevail!"

When the Conservatives claimed that the Lords was the watchdog of the constitution, Lloyd-George, for the Liberals, weighed in scornfully that it was *"Mr. Balfour's Poodle"*: The Lords was *it fetches and carries for him and barks and bites anybody he sets it on to.* Churchill took his attack on the Lords further, describing them as:

a one-sided hereditary, unprized, unrepresentative, irresponsible absentee.

This almost amounted to a "class" attack, and went beyond what Balfour thought of his tactics. Since politics is about power, and having lost his power in 1906, he had to use what weapons were available to him in the struggle against the Liberal administration. It was a dangerous game, but it was party politics.

The Liberal resolution passed very easily, but a resolution has no legal or constitutional effect. The Government had tried to warn off the Lords from their course of action. The resolution merely reflected a stage in the political battle: each side had tested its ground! At that stage the Liberals did not want to press the Lords' reform. When ill-health and death removed Campbell-Bannerman in 1908, Asquith became Prime Minister, with Lloyd George, Chancellor of the Exchequer, and Winston Churchill at the Board of Trade.

Though the Liberals could not claim as much success as they had hoped for, owing to the tactical skill of the Conservatives in the Lords, there were still some achievements to record between 1906 and 1908. These included the Trades Disputes Act, which ensured that Trade Unions would not in future be held responsible for damages resulting from a peaceful strike; a Coal Mines Act which established the eight-hour day in the mines; the Port of London Authority Act; a School Meals Act; a Merchant Shipping Act; a Workmen's Compensation Act; a Prevention of Crimes Act, which largely set up the Borstal system for young offenders; an Education Act in 1907 which set up the school medical service; and a Children's Act which established juvenile courts and remand homes for young offenders. Above all these, however, two measures dominated the scene.

In 1908 Asquith introduced a scheme for Old Age Pensions. It provided five shillings a week for single people and seven shillings and sixpence for married couples, on condition that their other income was less than £26 a year or £39 for a married couple. The qualifying age was 70 years. General taxation would cover the cost, not an insurance scheme. This was the first time that a "cash handout" from the State was received as of right by any segment of the population: it was a modest grant and cost, in the first financial year, £6 million.

The same years had seen Churchill establish a network of Labour Exchanges in an attempt to alleviate unemployment. It cannot be said, therefore, that the Conservatives in the Lords hindered all governmental initiatives: the Conservatives simply exercised their considerable political skill with the view that it would not take too long to woo the electorate back to conservatism, and in 1908 by-election successes seemed to confirm this.

The Liberals, on the other hand, grew increasingly aware that few measures of importance had been passed without the personal blessing of Balfour and his lordly ally, Lansdowne.

*For three years the smallest opposition within living memory had effectively
decided what could and what could not be passed through Parliament.*[3]

While the Liberals grew exasperated with the Lords' conduct, they
had to face up to the fearful reality of Germany's plans for naval
expansion. The First Sea Lord, Sir John Fisher, after bitter debate in
the Cabinet, pushed the government into a building programme for
eight Dreadnought class warships. The cost of these, some £11 million,
and the cost of the Old Age Pensions, required the Chancellor, Lloyd
George, to raise about £16 million additional revenue in his People's
Budget of 1909. There is little to suggest that the measures to raise the
money were designed by Lloyd George to provoke a clash with the
Lords, but the possibility of such was well known to him and his
Cabinet colleagues. Few people thought, in fact, that the Lords would
be mad enough to reject a Money Bill.

How was the extra £16 million to be raised? Lloyd George
decided to increase Death Duties on estates over £5000 and income tax
from 1s. to 1s. 2d. in the £, and introduced a super tax of 6d. in the £
on the sum by which all incomes of £5000 or more exceeded £3000.
Heavier taxes were imposed on tobacco and spirits, and liquor licence
duties were increased. There was also to be a tax on motor cars and
petrol to contribute to a road-building fund. But what stirred up all
the trouble were the Land taxes—a duty of 20 per cent on the un-
earned increment of Land values was to be paid whenever land
changed hands, and also a duty of ½d. in the £ on the capital value of
undeveloped land and minerals.

For Lloyd George it was:

*a war Budget for raising money to wage implacable warfare against
poverty and squalidness.*

He had long held that the condition of the people demanded radical,
socialistic remedies.

Public opinion was stirred. Banner headlines announced the
People's Budget: in the Daily Mail,

Plundering the Middle Class

and in the Daily Express,

Socialist Budget. What You Will Have to Pay.

In the Commons the Conservatives launched immediately into battle.
One member saw the Budget as:

the beginning of the end of all rights of property,

while Balfour attacked it as:

*vindictive, inequitable, based on no principle, and injurious to the
productive capacity of the country.*

THE LAND

Why do the Lords refuse to pass the Budget?

They give plenty of excuses, but everybody knows that one of the real reasons is that the Budget taxes land values.

The Tory cry is—"HANDS OFF THE LAND!"

The Liberal policy is—TAXATION OF LAND VALUES AND THE BEST USE OF THE LAND IN THE INTERESTS OF THE COMMUNITY.

A Liberal party leaflet of 1909

Almost all parliamentary time was taken up as the Commons debated the proposals.

In the country, the fiery eloquence of Lloyd George and Churchill reached great heights as they defended the Budget and attacked the Conservative tactics. Naturally the House of Lords issue was raised again, and, with it, the class war. In July 1909 at Limehouse, Lloyd George had challenged:

> [The Lords] *are forcing a revolution. The Peers may decree a revolution but the people will direct it. If they begin, issues will be raised that they little dream of. Questions will be asked which are now whispered in humble voice, and answers will be demanded with authority.*

Asquith, meanwhile, had kept a low profile which contrasted with that of Lloyd George and Churchill. The Press in the form of *The Times* was perplexed:

> *by the contrast between the utterances of the Prime Minister and those of his most active lieutenants . . . openly preaching the doctrine that rich men have no right to their property, and that it is the proper function of Government to take it from them . . . which of these voices is the real voice of the government?*

If *The Times* was doubting, Lloyd George was not. At Newcastle in October 1909 he issued a powerful warning to the Lords, whom he described as:

> *500 men, ordinary men chosen accidentally from among the unemployed,*

not to meddle any longer with the progress of the Budget through Parliament. He thundered:

> *they have no qualification—at least they need not have any. They do not have to have a medical certificate . . . they only require a certificate of birth —just to prove they are first of the litter. You would not choose a spaniel on these principles.*

It was strange that he was attacking the party of conservatism for revolutionary attitudes.

The political sparring went on in both Houses right through until, in November 1909, the Lords rejected the Budget—the first time a finance bill had been rejected for over two hundred and fifty years—by 350 to 75 votes.

The Commons retaliated with another Liberal resolution condemning the Lords' action, which the Prime Minister, Asquith, called:

> *a breach of the constitution and usurpation of the rights of the Commons.*

Lloyd George put it simply and optimistically:

> *their greed has overcome their craft and we have got them.*

Asquith took the issue to the people by calling a General Election for January 1910.

This was the beginning of the great constitutional struggle that dispels any myth of political stability and quietude that may be the impression lent by distance to the Edwardian era. Despite the cry of "Peers against the People", the main issue of the election remained the Budget of 1909. During the campaign Asquith misled many people

by giving the impression that King Edward VII had agreed to create sufficient Liberal peers to achieve a balance in the House of Lords; in fact the King had not. While the Conservatives lost all the seats that had been regained in the by-elections between 1907 and 1909, they won 116 seats and became the majority party in England. Scotland and Wales overwhelmingly supported the Liberals but the landslide advantage of 1906 had slipped well away. The Liberal majority over Conservative was only two seats. The composition of the new House of Commons was:

Liberals	275
Conservatives	273
Labour	40
Irish Nationalists	85

The Liberals' working majority could only be achieved with Labour and Irish support.

For Asquith the problem that pestered him was what course to follow, especially as regards the House of Lords; and it was made worse by his mishandling of the issue of creation of peers. On 21 February 1910 he admitted to the Commons:

I have received no such guarantee and I have asked for no such guarantee.

Liberals felt cheated and many advised Asquith and his ministers to resign. He did not, but the administration remained shaken and depressed.

On 14 April 1910, the Liberals introduced, as expected, the Parliament Bill to limit the power of the House of Lords. It had three main provisions:

1. the Lords could not in future amend or reject a Money Bill (with the Speaker to decide which measures qualified);
2. if a Bill were rejected by the Lords it would become law provided that not less than 2 years elapsed between the introduction in the Commons and its third reading there;
3. the maximum duration of Parliaments should be reduced to 5 years instead of 7.

Meanwhile the Lords, accepting the decision of the electorate, passed the Budget without a division.

The decision of whether or not the Lords would accept the Parliament Bill was still open when, on 6 May 1910, King Edward VII died suddenly after a short illness. His successor, George V, was hard-working and dedicated, but hopelessly ill-prepared to deal with the difficulties of a constitutional crisis. For five months the party leader-

Prime Minister Asquith surrounded by the problems that shattered the calm of the Edwardian era.

ships discussed the Parliament Bill in a constitutional conference but it finally broke down over the Conservatives' suggestion that all constitutional legislation, if rejected twice by the Lords, should be tested by a national referendum. By November, the Cabinet, frustrated by the lack of progress on Lords' reform, decided to go to the country again. After tense discussion and many misgivings, King George was persuaded by Asquith that if necessary he *would* create enough peers to see the Reform Bill through the Lords, if the people wished it. The King wrote:

> *I disliked having to [make peers] . . . very much, but agreed that it was the only alternative to the Cabinet resigning, which at this moment would be disastrous.*

Naturally public interest in the second general election of 1910 fell noticeably, but Lloyd George's rantings again stirred up controversy:

> *an aristocracy is like cheese: the older it is the higher it becomes.*

But the election result was a further weakening of the Liberal position:

Liberals	272
Conservatives	272
Labour	42
Irish Nationalists	87

The next eight months witnessed bitter political warfare over the Parliament Bill, and only after 800 Conservative amendments had been defeated, did the measure pass the Commons. Still the uncertainty of the Lords remained. Through the hot summer of 1911 a kind of madness gripped the Conservative extremists especially in the Lords, under the leadership of the 87-year-old Earl of Halsbury. However, by August, with the knowledge that the government had drawn up a list of 500 new peers, the Lords, after an exceedingly bitter debate on the 9th and 10th, passed the Parliament Bill by 131 to 114 votes.

The Liberals had won the constitutional battle that had raged from 1906, but what had been gained? They had gained a measure of Lords' reform, opening the way to speedier passage of much needed social legislation, but the Liberals had, in the struggle, lost their superiority in the Commons by 1910. Conservative tactics, while they had paid off till 1909, were now considered disreputable. The infant Labour Party had made significant progress mostly at Liberal expense and the Irish Nationalists were now in a position to call the political tune.

---

[1]*The Supreme Command* by Lord Hankey (ALLEN & UNWIN, 1961); [2]*The British Revolution* by R. Rhodes James (HAMISH HAMILTON, 1976); [3]*Mr Balfour's Poodle* by R. Jenkins (COLLINS, 1954)

5

Another Irish Crisis

The Edwardians inherited from the Victorians all the complexities and difficulties that composed the Irish Question. While the Conservative party had adopted the label "Unionist" to symbolize their policy that the Act of Union of 1800, which bound Ireland to the rest of the United Kingdom, ought to be preserved intact, the Liberal Party had twice, in 1886 and 1893, been persuaded by Gladstone to attempt (both times in vain) Home Rule for Ireland. When the Edwardian age dawned, Liberalism still inclined, though more cautiously than under Gladstone, to keep Irish Home Rule a future possibility. In the twenty years preceding the Liberal government of 1906, the Irish question had become quiescent; two factors had accounted for this. Irish Nationalism failed to find a leader with the charismatic brilliance or political skill of Parnell. Unionist governments had attempted to *"kill Home Rule by kindness"*, and to apply what Salisbury called *"resolute government"*. Most important was the solution of the rankling land question by means of Wyndham's Land Purchase Act of 1903.

In the first four years of their ministry the Liberals adopted a "step by step" policy which tried by limited reforms, to ameliorate the grievances of the Irish and, at the same time, to move the British public towards future acceptance of Home Rule. Legislation passed included local government reorganization, the end of coercion, more protection for evicted tenants, housing and educational improvements as well as the encouragement of the Irish language and the foundation of the National University of Ireland and the Queen's University of Belfast by the Universities Act of 1908. Ireland, too, had benefited from Old Age Pensions. All these measures convinced the British public that the troublesome Irish question was settled. According to Lord Midleton,

Ireland in 1906 had never been so quiet for six hundred years.
And Constantine Fitzgibbon has written:

This period of Ireland's history has a flavour that lingers and enchants . . .
Happiness seemed at last to be taking root in Irish soil.[1]
But this was a superficial impression.

Irish nationalism now concentrated its energies in the single issue of independence. But the politics of independence was complex. Ranged alongside the Nationalist group of M.P.s at Westminster, never less than eighty during the Liberal administration, and the Irish Republican Brotherhood, the Fenians, there was from 1905 Sinn Fein, ("Ourselves Alone") founded by Arthur Griffith and clear in its dedication to *"the re-establishment of the independence of Ireland"*. To Sinn Fein, Home Rule did not mean independence. Griffith wrote that Home Rulers might acknowledge Britain's right to govern their country, but:

> *the Nationalist on the other hand totally rejects the claim of England,*
> *or any other country, to rule over or interfere with the destinies of Ireland.*

The Irish Republican Brotherhood, by the early years of this century, had grown increasingly inactive, and remained so until about 1910.

At Westminster the eighty or so Irish M.P.s, who formed the Nationalist group, had by 1900 come under the leadership of John Redmond. He was no Parnell, but nevertheless the party commanded support from the majority of the Irish people. But while the party spoke for most of Ireland, it seemed at times to neglect or underestimate the underlying trends of Irish society. Throughout the period Irish national consciousness had been roused. There were several elements in this.

Michael Cusack had founded in 1884 the Gaelic Athletic Association to lead Irish youth away from their subservience to "foreign" or British games. It was remarkably successful; by 1890 it had more than 50,000 members who became intensely proud of their "Irishness" and resentful of the union with Britain. The formation in 1893 of the Gaelic League, and the remarkable Irish literary revival at the turn of the century, were other signs of a new form of Irish Nationalism. By 1906, 100,000 members had flocked to join the League's activities, which embraced the promotion of Irish language, history, drama, music and dancing, as an "adult education-cum-entertainment movement." The neglect of Irish and Irish history in the educational system was attacked. In 1904 only 104 schools taught Irish; by 1906 this had risen to 3000. And in 1912 the National University stipulated Irish as a compulsory entrance subject. The League even forced the closure of the pubs on St Patrick's Day, turned that day into a national holiday, and promoted native industry by organizing industrial parades. While it is difficult to weigh up exactly the Gaelic League's political contribution, it was described by Patrick Pearse in 1914 as *the most revolutionary influence that has ever come into Ireland.* Indeed many of the young men who later led Sinn Fein and the I.R.B. came into politics through the Gaelic League.

A separate and distinct Irish culture was now seen as an indispensable element in any meaningful independence. In contrast to the Gaelic League, the revival of Irish literature was not in Irish at all! It was in English and was rooted in the west of Ireland. Its main figures were Lady Gregory, Edward Martyn, George Moore, W. B. Yeats and J. M. Synge: and only Martyn was a Catholic. As a circle they made a deliberate attempt to cross the traditional barriers of religion and politics and to work for a united Irish nation with a genuine culture. Despite their depth of commitment, the writers had rather limited appeal to their contemporaries. Nevertheless, they must be given credit for revitalizing Irish literature and putting the Abbey Theatre, Dublin, on the world's drama map.

Another element in the promotion of Irish consciousness came in the early years of the century through the activities of the Irish trade unions. In the forefront of working-class politics were Jim Larkin and James Connolly who organized the Irish Transport and General Workers' Union. While they sought to improve wages and social conditions, independence for Ireland was a vital part of the programme. As Connolly wrote:

The cause of Labour is the cause of Ireland, the cause of Ireland is the cause of Labour.

Ireland had had its share of economic improvement in the Edwardian years, especially in rural areas where long term loans had been made available (1903) so that peasants could buy land holdings. But urban poverty remained appalling. Conditions in the slums of Belfast and Dublin were among the worst in Europe. "Dear, dirty Dublin" had 21,000 families living in single-room tenements. Wages were still very low. Dublin's death-rate was 27.6 per 1000 in 1911, the highest of any capital in Europe.

Marx, Engels and Lenin had each kept a close eye on Ireland, and had predicted that when the socialist revolution came to the world, it might well be sparked off in Ireland. When, in the summer of 1913, there was a long and bitter strike, first of Dublin tramworkers, and then of all the T. & G. W. Union members in the commercial empire of the wealthy industrialist, William Martin Murphy, some European socialists believed the socialist revolution had begun. Not so, but the strike developed into a lockout when Murphy organized about 400 employers into a Federation to force a showdown with the Union. In all 24,000 people were locked out. There were violent clashes between strikers and the police and on 31 August, when Larkin was addressing a crowd in Dublin, the police turned on them with their batons. Two people were killed and hundreds—including 200 policemen—were injured. As a result the Union set up the Irish Citizen Army for its protection—an ominous development as time would prove.

In Ireland then, behind the more or less peaceful front, lurked a nationalist dynamic one, fomented by a number of groups and influences—the literary movement, the Gaelic League, the G.A.A., Sinn Fein, the I.R.B. and the Labour movement—each devoted to some social, cultural or political ideal, but taken together they rekindled the desire for independence in the minds of Irishmen.

In 1905 there had been little mention of Home Rule in the Liberals' programme, and between 1906 and 1910 they made no move towards its achievement. But the election results of 1910 removed their majority and their continuance in power depended on Irish Nationalist support. Redmond put his party's bargaining position clearly in a letter he wrote to Morley:

> Unless a declaration of Home Rule be made, not only will it be impossible for us to support Liberal candidates in England, but we will most unquestionably have to ask our friends to vote against them . . . as you know very well, the opposition of Irish voters in Lancashire, Yorkshire and other places, including Scotland, would certainly mean the loss of many seats.

The Liberals decided to pay the price—Home Rule. And so, they were pushed back to the issue that had wrecked them in 1886 and kept them out of power for, more or less, the next twenty years. Most ministers remained at best lukewarm in their commitment to Home Rule, though Churchill had, in 1908, stated at Manchester:

> the Liberal Party should claim full authority and a full hand to deal with the problem of Irish self-government without being restricted to a mere measure of administrative devolution.

Prime Minister Asquith had moved quite a lot from the attitude he had expressed in 1902:

> Is it to be part of the policy and programme of our party that, if returned to power, it will introduce into the House of Commons a bill for Irish Home Rule? The answer, in my judgement, is No.

but he never became more than lukewarm. His decision to introduce the Bill in 1910 was based on political considerations rather than on principle. The Unionists, on the other hand, could not be expected to

The Liberal Government in 1910 became dependent for its survival on the support of the Irish Nationalists, who thus called the "Home Rule" tune. Here Redmond, the Nationalist leader, leads Asquith, Lloyd George and Churchill by the nose. From which side did this propaganda come?

condone the Liberals' attitude. Political considerations *and* principle determined their actions. It seemed that the Liberals were being black-mailed by the Nationalists into Home Rule, a constitutional change for which they had no mandate. Also the anxieties of their supporters in Ulster convinced them that Home Rule had to be opposed tooth and nail.

In the nine counties that formed the historic province of Ulster there were, according to the 1911 census, 687,000 (43.6 per cent of the population) Roman Catholics and 889,000 (56.4 per cent) Protestants of all persuasions. In parts of Ulster, such as Belfast and the Counties Down and Antrim, the Protestants outnumbered the R.C.s by as much as two to one. In others, like Cavan, Donegal and Monaghan, the reverse was true. The other four counties were evenly balanced. These figures, while their reality ought to destroy the arguments of the bigots, did nothing to remove the religious antagonism between Protestants and Catholics. It was enough for most Ulster-men that Home Rule meant Rome Rule. Extreme Unionists in Belfast proclaimed that loyalist "Protestant" Ulster was about to be sold in bondage to the disloyal "Catholic" portion of the island. Such was Ulster Unionist fervour that Bonar Law, who became leader of the Conservatives at Westminster in 1911, claimed: *"these people are . . . prepared to die for their convictions."*

It was not until April 1912 that the Prime Minister, Asquith, introduced the third Home Rule Bill into the Commons. He did so with little enthusiasm and many misgivings. John Redmond, leader of the Irish Nationalist Party, however, greeted it enthusiastically:

> I believe it will put an end once and for all to the wretched ill-will, suspicion and disaffection that have existed in Ireland, and to the suspicion and misunderstanding that have existed between this country and Ireland.

The great mass of the Irish people agreed with him. But not the leaders of Ulster Unionism. Ulster would not be ruled by the South.

The leaders of the Conservative Party decided to back Ulster's determination. At a political rally at Blenheim Palace on 29 July 1912, while the Bill was on its first passage through the Commons, Bonar Law shattered the political conventions of the time by declaring that, if a Dublin Parliament was forced on Ulster,

> I can imagine no length of resistance to which Ulster can go in which I should not be prepared to support them, and in which, in my belief, they would not be supported by the overwhelming majority of the British people.

Bonar Law, with his Presbyterian upbringing and personal connections with Ulster, was the first leader of his party to understand and sympathize with the stubborn Ulstermen. He was "passionately concerned" that the rights of the Protestant minority had to be protected.

Ulster's reaction to the introduction of the Bill was immediately hostile. In September 1911 Sir Edward Carson, the Ulster Unionist leader at Westminster, warned an audience in Belfast:

> We must be prepared, the morning Home Rule passes, ourselves to become responsible for the government of the Protestant province of Ulster.

By January 1912 a Volunteer force of Ulstermen had started drilling; on 9 April Carson, Lord Londonderry and Law took the salute at a march past of 80,000 Orange Volunteers. For the Liberals, Churchill spoke out courageously in Belfast at a Home Rule meeting in March:

> The flame of Irish nationality is inextinguishable.

During the summer of 1912 sectarian violence flared in Ulster. A Protestant Sunday School outing was attacked by Catholics at Castledawson in County Londonderry; in the Belfast shipyard, the largest in the world and where the ill-fated Titanic was built, reprisals were taken against Catholics; serious fighting took place at a football match between Celtic and Linfield—traditional sectarian rivals. Meetings of Unionists took place throughout the Province, culminating in September with a great rally in the Ulster Hall, Belfast, at which Carson roused the audience to pass the simple resolution:

> We will not have Home Rule.

More than 100 people were hurt when fighting broke out between Catholic and Protestant football supporters at the match between Belfast Celtic and Linfield at Celtic's ground, 14 September 1912.

On 28 September he led a huge procession to the City Hall in Belfast to sign a Solemn League and Covenant:

to defeat the present conspiracy to set up a Home Rule Parliament in Ireland.

The vast crowd was admitted to sign the document in batches of 500 at a time; 150 signed every minute and signing went on very late into the evening. In all 471,414 people signed the Covenant that day. Many of these developments in Ulster were wholeheartedly supported by the Conservatives. F. E. Smith, for instance, declared at Lincoln:

with Ulster undoubtedly in arms . . . I tell you that Ulster will not stand alone.

and a backbencher, Colonel Hickman, stated:

personally they have all my sympathies . . . when the time comes if there is any fighting to be done—I am going to be in it.

Action in Ulster was matched by long, rancorous debates at Westminster. As the Liberals, supported by the Nationalists, pushed on with their Bill and with the Conservatives opposing every detail and putting forward amendments, the question of partition began to be mooted. Redmond was convinced that the Nationalists would not accept Home Rule without Ulster: Ireland simply could not survive economically without the industries of Ulster. He argued,

Ireland is for us one entity. It is one land.

Carson attempted an amendment which sought to leave out Ulster since he believed that the Government would find home rule imposs-ible without Ulster. But the amendment was lost by 97 votes. Carson warned that if the Government pushed on and coerced Ulster it would be tantamount to a declaration of war and if so, Ulster was not "*altogether unprepared.*" For the Conservatives, Law insisted,

> . . . *if Ulster does resist by force, there are stronger influences than Parliamentary majorities . . . no Government would dare to use their troops to drive them out.*

In public, a few days later, he reiterated his position:

> *In our opposition to them [Government and supporters] we shall not be guided by the considerations or bound by the restraints which would influence us in an ordinary constitutional struggle. We shall take the means, whatever means seem to us most effective, . . .*
>
> *I said the other day in the House of Commons, and I repeat here, that there are things stronger than Parliamentary majorities.*

Asquith blandly refused to believe that civil war was threatening. In Dublin he said,

> *I tell you quite frankly that I do not believe in the prospect of civil war*

and advocated that the opposition would accept what he called

> *the supreme authority of the Imperial Parliament.*

Churchill, in a letter to *The Times,* took up the cudgels and argued:

> *Mr Bonar Law and his lieutenant, Sir Edward Carson, have . . . incited the Orangemen to wage civil war . . . In a constitutionally governed*

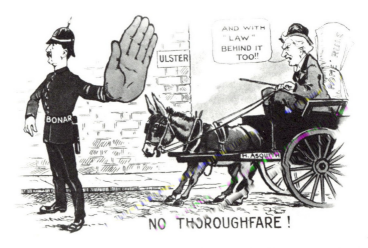

NO THOROUGHFARE !

Unionist propaganda—with a pun on the Opposition leader's name. In the original the hand is red—why would this have been appropriate?

country . . . there is no need and no excuse for violence . . . All this talk of violence, of bayonets and bullets, of rebellion and civil war has come from one side alone.

Debates became quite violent. On one occasion the Speaker was forced to suspend the House and on another, a prominent Ulster M.P., Mr Ronald MacNeill, hit Churchill on the forehead with a copy of the Standing Orders. On 13 January 1913, the third reading of the Bill was passed by the Commons by a majority of 110. On 30 January it was, as had been foreseen, thrown out by the Lords by 326 to 69 votes. On 10 March a new Session began, and the Bill started all over again. On 7 July it received its third reading in the Commons, but on 15 July the Lords again rejected it. Thus when the end of the session came in August 1913 the Home Rule Bill had been twice passed by the Commons and twice rejected by the Lords. Under the terms of the Parliament Act, it could not be long delayed: in fact it was bound to become law by the summer of 1914.

As the debates raged in parliament, the situation in Ulster became more serious. The Ulster Volunteers, now under the command of a retired army officer, General George Richardson, grew from 56,000 men in September 1913 to 84,000 by March 1914. A provisional government was ready to take over in Ulster as soon as home rule became law. Carson, the Ulster leader understood exactly the position that had emerged:

I am told it will be illegal. Of course it will. Drilling is illegal . . . the Volunteers are illegal and the Government know they are illegal, and the Government dare not interfere with them . . . Don't be afraid of illegalities.

Despite the gravity of the situation the Liberal government continued to play down the threat of civil war. Chief Secretary for Ireland, Augustine Birrell, admitted,

That there is great perturbation is certain; and the notion that it is all bluff may be dismissed. Personally I cannot bring myself to believe in civil war, even in its mildest terms.

The Nationalists, too, seemed convinced that the Ulstermen were bluffing. Joe Devlin, the Nationalist M.P. for West Belfast, declared in February 1914,

We do not believe in the reality of the threats of civil war indulged in by Sir Edward Carson and his followers, and we are convinced that the danger is grotesquely exaggerated.

Treating Ulster separately was not, up to this point, considered very seriously by the Liberals. Indeed as far as the Conservatives were concerned they were content to lose Home Rule completely on account of the special position of Ulster. Carson was more sanguine: Home Rule he still felt could not be prevented by Ulster but Ulster would not be part of it! By this time, too, the King, George V, had become alarmed at the deteriorating situation in Ireland and had been advised by Bonar Law that he ought to dissolve Parliament since the Liberals did not have a mandate for Home Rule. While the King rejected this part of Law's advice, he was even more worried by Law's other question on the loyalty of the Army in Ireland—if Home Rule was to be imposed on Ulster by force, would the Army obey? The King's anxiety was increased by the passionate letters of loyalty that he received from the ordinary citizens of Ulster. The reiterated cry was,

Surely the King is not going to hand us over to the Pope?

Finally in mid-August 1913 the King suggested to his Prime Minister, Asquith, that an all-party conference ought to be arranged and should consider not only giving some form of devolution to Ulster, but to Wales and Scotland as well. Asquith, though not opposed in principle to a conference, thought that an *"unbridgeable chasm of principle"* existed between the two sides. But in the late autumn of 1913 the King had his way and talks between Asquith and Bonar Law took place. They met several times to investigate whether and if so how, Ulster could be excluded from the Home Rule Bill. In March 1914, moving the third reading of the Bill in the Commons, Asquith indicated that the government was prepared to allow any Ulster county to opt out of a Home Rule Parliament for six years. Redmond, while resolutely opposed to partition, accepted the temporary arrangement. But Carson was enraged:

We do not want sentence of death with a stay of execution for six years.

The Government, however, persisted with this amendment, but when the Bill went finally to the Lords in June 1914 the Unionist peers forced another amendment which allowed for the permanent exclusion of Ulster.

Deadlock had been reached. To break it the King summoned an all-party conference to meet at Buckingham Palace on 20 July 1914. The Government was represented by the Prime Minister and Lloyd George; the Opposition by Bonar Law and Lord Lansdowne; Ulster by Sir Edward Carson and Captain J. Craig; and the Irish Nationalists by Redmond and Dillon. Difficulties were met right away: no agreement could be reached over the geographical limits of Ulster, particularly on whether Fermanagh and Tyrone were to be included or not. The Speaker, who had chaired the conference, reported to the King that, *"being unable to agree, either in principle or in detail"*, the conference had broken down. It had lasted only four days. The date was 24 July 1914.

In Ireland the months of tepid negotiation, through April to July, had witnessed increasing trouble; paramilitary forces north and south prepared for the worst. Smuggling had contributed some arms and ammunition to Ulster but it was not until April 1914 that the *S.S. Clyde Valley* landed 30,000 German rifles and 3 million rounds of ammunition at Larne, Bangor and Donaghadee for use by the Ulster Volunteers. As if this was not bad enough news for the Liberal Government, it came on top of the anxiety created a month before by the Curragh incident. A number of British army officers, stationed at the Curragh, near Dublin, had announced that they would rather resign their commissions than move against Ulster. Meantime in the South a steady trickle of arms was coming in mostly from America. In July 1914 Nationalist Volunteers carried out a gun-running operation at Howth and Kilcoole. In broad daylight 1500 rifles and 58,000 rounds were landed, largely as a result of the work of Protestant sympathizers with the Nationalist cause. The money had been raised by a committee in London which included Sir Roger Casement. The arms were purchased in Hamburg, and transported to Ireland in two yachts belonging to members of the Anglo-British gentry. The Nationalist Volunteers were recruiting hard and by July 1914 had reached 160,000—more than 40,000 of them were in Ulster, with the stated objective:

to secure and maintain the rights and liberties of all the people of Ireland.

Dublin, itself, was in a ferment and troops were called out to quell the restlessness. An angry crowd stoned them and in the mêlée three civilians were shot and 38 wounded. Ireland was on the brink of civil war.

Suddenly Irish affairs were pushed into the background by news from Europe. On 4 August 1914 Britain declared war on Germany. This virtually killed the Home Rule Bill. Though it received the Royal Assent on 18 September 1914, its operation was suspended until the end of the war and Asquith promised the introduction of another amending bill to cater for Ulster. "Cold storage" was no lasting solution to a problem that had for so long generated so much heat. Easter 1916 was to provide yet another twist to the tragic story of Ireland.

---

¹*Out of the Lion's Paw* by C. Fitzgibbon (MACDONALD, 1969)

6

Wiles of Women

The political turmoil of Edwardian Britain, which gives the lie to the superficial calm veneer so devotedly described by some memoir-writers, was accompanied, certainly in the latter half of the era, by not a little hysteria. By 1910 government ministers had been forced to curtail their public appearances and security precautions had been improved for their protection. Indeed in 1912 rumours circulated of assassination attempts planned against the Prime Minister, Asquith, and the Chancellor of the Exchequer, Lloyd George; a hatchet had been flung at the Prime Minister during a visit to Dublin and the Chancellor's new house at Walton Heath was badly damaged by fire. In both cases arrests were made; and the culprits were women! In their defence the women claimed that they had been provoked by the Liberal government's refusal to extend the parliamentary vote to women. They, in fact, were militant campaigners for "Votes for Women", the movement led by Mrs Emmeline Pankhurst that contributed some hysteria to the turmoil of the late Edwardian political scene. Her ambition was to improve the lot of women in society:

> It is our duty to make this world a better place for women . . . if we get the vote, it will mean changed conditions for our less fortunate sisters.

This Suffragette movement was but one aspect of the role of women in Edwardian Britain. At the outset, however, it should be pointed out that the relationship between men and women remained much as it ever was and that it was Edwardian newspapers and magazines that developed the misconception that women of that era were liberating themselves from the shackles of Victorianism. For instance, under the pseudonym "A spinster" in the *Lady's Realm*, was written the "Englishman's usual notion of womanhood":

> a being of inferior intellect, a creature of caprice to be humoured and petted and deceived.

This kind of provocation probably made the Edwardian lady of leisure smile gently and push her to even greater exertions in the giddy social round that was "the Season". Household management took up just a little time and the rest was left to fashionable dressing, playing bridge, paying calls and leaving cards, preparing for weekend house parties, dinner parties and dances. Vera Brittain described life in 1912 and 1913:

> *I went to more dances, paid calls, skated and tobogganed, played a good deal of bridge and a great deal of tennis and golf, had music lessons and acted in amateur theatricals; in fact I passed my days in all those conventional pursuits with which the leisured young woman of every generation has endeavoured to fill the time that she is not qualified to use.*[1]

This was certainly the pattern of the female role for the upper and middle classes, and few had Vera Brittain's perspicacity to understand its lack of intellectual or social satisfaction.

The same feeling is echoed in H. G. Wells's *Ann Veronica* (1909):

> *"Then I suppose when I have graduated I am to come home?"*
> *"It seems the natural course."*
> *"And do nothing?"*
> *"There are plenty of things a girl can find to do at home."*[2]

In March 1913 Vera Brittain wrote:

> *It feels sad to be a woman! . . . Men seem to have so much more choice as to what they are intended for.*[1]

While Vera Brittain fought on to make a career for herself, the social convention of the female role in that class remained:

> *She [Vera's mother] was invariably tackled by one or two stalwart middle class mothers who did not hesitate to tell her how deplorable they thought my future plans.*
> *"How can you send your daughter to college, Mrs Brittain?" moaned one lugubrious lady. "Don't you want her ever to get married?"*[1]

The same conventional attitude to the female role is echoed in Cicely Hamilton's epithet of 1909:

> *Boys are to be happy in themselves: the girls are to make others happy.*

For most of the upper and middle classes, then, marriage and motherhood were still the socially prescribed goals for women and the key function of wife and mother was to provide a comfortable, well-run home for the family members. It was a narrow domestic role. Energy and talent could find their way out only in charity work. Only the extrovert few defied the socially accepted conventions.

But while the conventional role had not changed much, the opportunities open to women of the upper and middle classes had. This was not a sudden process, rather it was the product of trends in society, particularly in the latter part of the 19th century. There had been much intellectual, political and literary criticism of the narrowness of the female role, and educational facilities for girls and young women had been developed. Women novelists had appeared before the middle of the century, among them George Eliot, Mrs William Ellis and Harriet Martineau. Practical womanhood had its heroine in Florence Nightingale at the time of the Crimean War. Political organizations specially for women were formed by Liberals and Conservatives after the 1883 Corrupt Practices Act made organization of the electorate essential, while the Temperance movement and Josephine Butler's campaign against legalized prostitution kept women and their role in society in the forefront of political discussion throughout the eighties and nineties.

Educational opportunities for women had also, in the same period, developed, especially after the 1870 Act which expanded the State's role in the primary sector. By 1890 eighty schools had been founded on the model of Cheltenham Ladies College and by 1901 thirty-one schools modelled themselves on the North London Collegiate School. The pioneers of these were Miss Dorothea Beale and Miss Frances Buss. In the 1880s Oxford and Cambridge universities offered degrees to women students; the new civic universities had also done so. The education of girls was now a serious project, but not without infringement of the conventions of society. Women and marriage had also received considerable attention in the late 19th century: the Married Women's Property Act of 1883 was a milestone. It gave women power to sell or keep, if they wished, their real and personal possessions. But divorce law, particularly in relation to guardianship of children and sex relations, remained an issue for feminists right into the 20th century. Edward VII's own experiences in terms of the marriage question kept the issue alive: his affairs with Lily Langtry and Mrs Keppel were common knowledge, but accepted by society and by his wife. He took his own view:

It doesn't matter what you do, so long as you don't frighten the horses.

Despite that, on the appointment of women to the Royal Commission on Divorce in 1908 he criticized the Home Secretary on the grounds that divorce was a subject

which cannot be discussed openly and in all its aspects with any delicacy or even decency before Ladies.

Again the conventions of society persisted.

What was more significant, as regards women in society, than trends in intellectual argument, and moral and political attitudes, was the changing British economy. Growing numbers of women found themselves in employment. This was nothing new, since from 1850 over a third of the total workforce was female. But the number of women being attracted to a greater variety of jobs was new and this ran across the classes. After 1900 the "typewriter, telephone and department store" revolution hit Britain: it absorbed thousands of new women workers every year. By 1914 more than half a million women were at work in shops and offices.

Teaching and nursing expanded at the same time and 1914 saw nearly a quarter of a million women in these professions. The more traditional areas of female employment—textiles, clothing and food processing—also grew steadily. Domestic service employment declined slowly so that by 1914 the typical woman worker was no longer employed there. Such changes meant also that Trade Union membership among women tripled between 1900 and 1914, the figure then being 437,000. This social trend was reported in the *Sphere*:

There had grown up a race of bachelor girls in flats who live on caramels and sausages.

We have most decidedly changed for the better; the majority of unmarried girls now have their own employment and as long as they are not absolutely dependent on it for their bread they do very well.

Increasing job opportunity for females led to women being concerned in the improvement of wages and conditions of employment and to the search for more tangible acceptance of equality with men. The Edwardian period furnished adequate examples of these: the mill-working girls of Lancashire were swayed to swell the ranks of the Suffragettes mainly on the grounds that the vote for women would lead to betterment of wages and conditions of employment. At the same time, the period saw women take up interests in spheres where they had the chance to challenge and emulate the male of the species. The fair sex's interest in the motor car was one area where women reached towards equality. Sport was another: tennis, golf and roller-skating were taken up with relish by many Edwardian ladies. High fashion throughout the Edwardian period concentrated on utterly feminine frills and flounces and was founded on corsets. The Suffragettes, of course, condemned corsets as shackles on women. Yet in 1911 fashion seemed to have joined the movement for equality!

The vast majority of women were not Suffragettes nor were they particularly sympathetic to their cause. This was especially true of working-class women who considered politics a "luxury" suitable for men who had time to think, and rather resented, and certainly

THE SEX QUESTION.
(A study in Bond Street.)

Emancipation in fashion? (1911)

distrusted, the middle-class leaders who had had little struggle in their
lives. Such an attitude is summed up in a comment of 1911,

*I reckon they suffragettes wants half a dozen kids like this yer squad o'
mine. That'd steady 'em.*[3]

The demand for Votes for Women was nothing new in British
society. In 1866 during debate on the franchise clause of the Reform
Bill, a petition signed by 1499 women had been presented to parliament
but without success. Its rejection led to the foundation of the National
Society for Women's Suffrage (1868). Lydia Becker, its secretary,
drummed up support for Liberal M.P.s such as J. S. Mill, Jacob
Bright and Richard Cobden who presented private bills for female
enfranchisement. In fact bills were presented every year from 1870 to
1878 and from 1884 onwards, except 1899 and 1901. Considerable

support was usually gained for these bills: in 1904 the majority in favour of extending voting rights to women was 114 and in 1908 it reached 179. However none of these votes produced a tangible result. They were fated to die in a variety of ways: some were suppressed by the government of the day, by procedures so that they never reached voting stage; others were "lost", usually by Conservative governments, in the Commons; and some, while Liberal governments were in power and sympathetic, were not proceeded with owing to time or the opposition of the Lords. Indeed, other, more pressing problems, like Ireland, dominated the work of governments after 1884 to the exclusion of franchise reform in general.

When the Edwardian age dawned, therefore, little progress had been made towards female suffrage, and it had been increasingly difficult in the 1890s for Millicent Fawcett, who inherited the mantle of Lydia Becker, to hold together the various groups of agitating women who had formed the National Union of Women's Suffrage Societies in 1897. It was not surprising that Mrs Emmeline Pankhurst decided on a more positive approach in 1903 with the foundation of the Women's Social & Political Union, better known simply as the Suffragettes, to campaign for women to have a direct voice in Parliament and so improve the lot of women in society.

At the start, Mrs Pankhurst had supported the Independent Labour Party, thinking it sympathetic to votes for women and concerned about working class women's conditions. Soon she became convinced that:

[Labour politicians and T.U. officials] . . . are very ready to propose restrictions on working women's labour. There are some who advocate the entire exclusion of women, whether married or single, from certain industries. There are those who also desire to close wage earning occupations to married women.[4]

In some respects this was an echo of working-class opinion about the role of women and was reiterated by Mr W. J. Davis of the Brassworkers Union at a conference on Unemployment and the Provision of Meals for School Children in 1905 when he complained that the

time would come when the man would have to stay at home and mind the baby and the woman would go out to work.

Mrs Pankhurst retorted:

if men had to stay at home to look after the babies, there would not be so many babies.

But this banter was typical of the first two years of the W.S.P.U. It attracted little attention and politicians and press chose mostly to ignore it. Although one M.P., Henry Labouchere, said in the Commons on 16 March 1904:

Women were too impulsive; they had too much heart, and were too good for political life.

And he stated baldly what he, and many other men thought:

The mission of a working man's wife was to look after the home, to mind the baby, to cook the dinner, and to do the household washing. She had no time for electioneering.

From 1905 the Suffragettes concentrated on marches and the interruption of political meetings to make politicians and the public aware of their case. But politicians were loathe to accept it. The political leaders of all parties, and especially the Conservatives and Liberals, were reluctant to grant women the vote mostly because of the uncertainty that a wider franchise would produce at elections. Also, Ireland, the House of Lords, and the fact that about 40 per cent of all adult males did not have the vote, were much more important than "votes for women".

Convincing individuals was just as difficult. Asquith's elevation to the Prime Ministership in April 1908 helped to clarify the official Liberal position—he was a stubborn opponent:

[Women] are for the most part hopelessly ignorant of politics. Credulous to the last degree, and flickering with gusts of sentiment like a candle in the wind.

The Liberal ministers, like the Conservative opposition leaders, were deeply divided on the issue. Grey, Lloyd George, Haldane, Birrell, Runciman and McKenna favoured franchise extension but varied in conviction. Balfour for the Tories found himself in that camp also. But Asquith, Harcourt, Burns, Samuel, and Churchill lined up as antis. F. E. Smith of the Tories produced one of the most devastating attacks on the Votes for Women campaign:

I venture to say that the total sum of human happiness, knowledge and achievement, would remain unaltered if . . . Sappho had never sung, Joan of Arc had never fought, Siddons had never played, and if George Eliot had never written.

By the summer of 1912, the Suffragettes had become completely frustrated by Government inaction. Three very contentious measures were then being considered: Home Rule for Ireland, Disestablishment of the Church of Wales, and Franchise & Registration—each bill demanded hard work and tight whipping. The Suffragettes hoped that the Franchise Bill would include an extension to include women. A further complication for the Government was the bitter dock strike in

Suffragette propaganda

London which began in late May. In other words, the Government had a great deal on its hands and many M.P.s regarded women's suffrage as a measure which had to be dispensed with or postponed. The situation provoked a hysterical response from the Suffragettes. But it ill-served their campaign. There was brawling in Parliament Square, window smashing in Piccadilly and Regent Street, at an India Office reception in June the Prime Minister was forcibly accosted by Suffragettes, although his wife, Margot, *"boxed the lady in the pink dress on the ears"*; in Dublin Asquith was narrowly missed and Redmond hit by a hatchet tossed by Mrs Mary Leigh into their open carriage. That same evening the redoubtable Mrs Leigh attempted to burn down the

Theatre Royal and, in due course, was sentenced to five years' penal servitude. In September Lloyd George had his golf at Llanystumdwy interrupted by Suffragettes. Suffragette flags were flown over the golf course at Balmoral, much to the annoyance of the Royal Family. Generally the campaign of militancy remained one of harassment rather than serious damage.

During that period the Liberal ministers, in Cabinet, decided to insert women's franchise clauses by an amendment in the Government Bill which sought to abolish plural voting and extend the male franchise, provided the measure was allowed a free vote in the Commons. Speaker Lowther, however, ruled in January 1913 against this move: since the amendment changed the Bill so much he decided that the Bill would have to be withdrawn and be re-introduced. It was a critical moment for the Cabinet, but generally the Government was relieved with an excuse to postpone votes for women; it felt it had too much on its plate at that time. John Burns put it more acidly:

Women Suffragists have by undisciplined action outside the Commons and in Cabinet put back for many years their own cause . . .

The end of the Franchise Bill, in fact, proved to be the last pre-war chance of procuring the Suffrage for Women. No militant believed that the Speaker's intervention was without Asquith's connivance and the public had to brace itself as militancy became hysterical.

Club windows were smashed in London, the Orchid House at Kew Gardens was wrecked, golf courses in Birmingham were attacked with acid. Some tenacious militants even went as far as to attempt to tear off Asquith's clothes while he golfed on the links at Lossiemouth. All such criminal acts were dealt with by the Law. Arrests were made, trials took place, often giving the Suffragettes even more publicity than they deserved, and sentences issued. Often the Suffragettes went to prison for non-payment of fines. There they continued to raise difficulties for the Government by going on hunger strike.

This forced the Government to sponsor the "Cat and Mouse" Act (1913) which allowed release for recuperation but followed this by rearrest. The fanaticism began to disgust even many friends of the women's cause. *"Diseased emotionalism"* was how the Manchester Guardian described it. Questions were asked about the mental and emotional stability of leading Suffragettes. Emily Davison, whose death at the 1913 Derby by bringing down the King's horse, Anmer, at Tattenham Corner, was perhaps the ultimate sacrifice for the movement, has since been described:

You wouldn't call Emily Davison a physically attractive person. She had a square face and a high complexion. Her voice was carrying and she used to speak "haw-haw" and they'd talk about "gels". But she was friendly to us office-girls, not standoffish. She was very learned with degrees and things. And she used to wear an academic gown and came to the office in a mortar board once. She had very starin' eyes and I used to say to Mary, a fellow office kid, that she was a bit unbalanced. I don't think it was suicide, but she knew it was a terrible risk—a 99% risk.[5]

In their writings, sloganizing and speeches, some of the Suffragettes give the impression of psychological abnormality.

THIS IS "THE HOUSE" THAT MAN BUILT,

AND these are a few of the women of note Who say that they want, and they will have the vote; And think that they ought, To have Man's support: Even although HE should have to go short, The sly Suffragette Who is all on the get And wants all, in THE HOUSE that man built.

Anti-Suffragette propaganda

How does one assess Mrs Pankhurst's slogan?

Votes for Women and Chastity for Men!

Or Mrs Pethick-Lawrence (1906):

It is a life and death struggle . . . What we are going to get is a great revolt of the women against their subjection of body and mind to men.

And how does one regard the outbursts of Christabel Pankhurst who claimed that three-quarters of all men had venereal disease, and that all physical relationships *"between the spiritually developed women of this new day and men who in thought and conduct with regard to sex matters are their inferiors"* must be abandoned.

These exorbitant claims provoked equally virulent attitudes from the anti-suffrage lobbies. The *Daily Express* reported that a Professor of Psychology, Dr Max Baff, who came from Massachusetts, had said:

All women are fundamentally savage, and the suffragist movement is simply an outbreak of emotional insanity.[5]

An eminent bacteriologist, Sir Almroth Wright, wrote to *The Times* on 28 March 1912:

No doctor can ever lose sight of the fact that the mind of woman is always threatened with danger from the reverberations of her physiological emergencies.

It was with such thoughts that the doctor lets his eyes rest upon the militant suffragist. He cannot shut them to the fact that there is mixed up with the woman's movement much mental disorder; and he cannot conceal from himself the physiological emergencies which lie behind.

Mrs Winston Churchill, sympathetic, but not extravagantly, to the Suffragette case, responded in another letter.

After reading Sir Almroth Wright's able and weighty exposition of women as he knows them, the question seems no longer to be "should women have votes?" but "Ought women not to be abolished altogether?" . . . we learn from him that in their youth they are unbalanced, that from time to time they suffer from unreasonableness and hypersensitiveness, and that their presence is distracting and irritating to men in their daily lives and pursuits. If they take up a profession, the indelicacy of their minds makes them undesirable partners of their male colleagues. Later on in life they are subject to grave and continued mental disorders, and if not quite insane, many of them have to be shut up . . . Cannot science give us some assurance, or at least some grounds of hope that we are on the eve of the greatest discovery of all, i.e. how to maintain a race of males by purely scientific means?

Mrs Churchill's counter-attack was lost on Sir Almroth, who published in 1913 *The Unexpurgated Case against Woman Suffrage* which contained gems like:

> *woman's mind . . . is over-influenced by individual instances; arrives at conclusions on incomplete evidence; has a very imperfect sense of proportion; accepts the congenial as true, and rejects the uncongenial as false.*[6]

and,

> *One would not be far from the truth if one alleged that there are no good women, but only women who have lived under the influence of good men.*[6]

Summing up the Suffragettes he asserted:

> *The failure to recognize that man is the master and why he is the master lies at the root of the Suffrage movement.*[6]

Such emotionalism was symptomatic of the aggravation felt by opponents of women's suffrage. It stemmed probably from the lack of political judgment shown by Mrs Pankhurst and her daughters, particularly when dissension appeared in the ranks and some of their leading colleagues deserted, and the indiscriminancy with which the Suffragettes chose their targets. Setting fire to public buildings, planting bombs in Westminster Abbey, smashing exhibits in the British Museum and damaging paintings, like the Rokeby Venus, in the National Gallery and the Royal Academy, did little to endear the Suffragettes to the public or politicians. More important is the effect the hysteria had on influential ministers, like Churchill and Lloyd George—it merely aggravated them. Lloyd George declared:

> *I have no desire to speak by gracious permission of Queen Christabel.*

Late in 1911 Churchill had reached the stage of calling for a referendum on the issue:

> *first to the women to know if they want it, and then to the men to know if they will give it.*

Mrs Pankhurst claimed in her memoirs, published in 1914, that militancy had been proved right because it had attracted attention.

> *. . . our heckling campaign made women's suffrage a matter of news . . . now the newspapers were full of us.*[4]

But the increasing violence and hysteria of the years 1911 to 1914 evoked anger not sympathy:

> *Edwardian Englishmen, seeing women rioting, burning, destroying property, and even dying, drew back in alarm from a cause that threatened to loose that rage for chaos upon the world of men. And since men governed England, it is not surprising that, after more than two decades of considering the problems of women, they went to war in 1914 with apparent relief, as a husband might leave a nagging wife, and left the problems unsolved, the liberating actions not even begun.*[7]

61

When war came, the Suffragettes patriotically stopped their agitation. All Suffragette prisoners were released; and encouraged by people like Christabel Pankhurst, women flocked to sign on for war work. To this call women of all classes rallied and did many kinds of jobs in the munition factories and in the field. Gradually the contributions made by women to the war effort established their right to full citizenship. The 1918 Representation of the People Act granted the vote to all men and to 8,500,000 women over 30. In the same year women were allowed to sit in the House of Commons.

Most suffrage supporters recognized the vote of 1918 as a tremendous victory, and others as a vital stage towards complete women's suffrage. Saying that the war brought votes for women is a crude generalization, but it contains some truth. The Editor of *The Times* in 1916 recognized this:

> *Time was when I thought that men alone maintained the state. Now I know that men alone never could have maintained it.*

While the Suffragette campaign had given ample publicity to the cause, female employment, and marriage and divorce changes cannot be overlooked in their contribution to the more liberal democratic atmosphere of the years just before 1914. There remained, however, two great barriers of prejudice in 1914: the hostility of men and the reluctance and opposition of many women. It was the war that broke down these barriers!

Overall, in the context of the Edwardian years, the Suffragette campaign, particularly in its militant aspect, is best regarded as a temporary nuisance rather than as a serious threat to the government of the country.

---

[1]Vera Brittain *op cit.*; [2]*Ann Veronica* by H. G. Wells (UNWIN, 1909); [3]*Seems So* by S. Reynolds (MACMILLAN, 1911); [4]*My Own Story* by E. Pankhurst (EVELEIGH NASH, 1914); [5]*Shoulder to Shoulder* (B.B.C. PUBLICATIONS, 1974); [6]*The Unexpurgated Case against Woman Suffrage* by Sir A. Wright (CONSTABLE, 1913); [7]*The Edwardian Turn of Mind* by S. Hynes (OXFORD, 1968)

7

Economic Complacency ?

*P*hrases such as "the age of extravagance", "the age of conspicuous consumption" and "the golden years", suggest that the Edwardian period was one of great economic prosperity. In fact, for some decades before 1914 Britain's economic position gave rise to serious concern as well as complacency.

In the world of 1870–80, major industrialization was still confined largely to Britain. Not only was she well in the lead as an economic power, she appeared to be enjoying an unending boom. Statistics for the period illustrate clearly Britain's healthy economic situation in relation to other states. In 1870, Britain produced more coal and iron than any other country; most of the world's goods were carried in British ships and the products of her factories entered the markets of the world, almost without restriction. Between 1849 and 1872 the value of her export trade quadrupled from £64 million to £256 million.

But the years of British supremacy were drawing to a close, and, slowly to begin with, then at an increasing rate, she came under serious challenge. This change was noted in a Treasury Minute of 1888:

Our position in the race of civilized nations is no longer what it has been. We have had a great start in industry and commerce, and by virtue of that start we have attained a station of unprecedented and long unchallenged supremacy. That supremacy is no longer unchallenged. Others are pressing on our heels.

By 1900 Germany had taken the lead in the metal industries and was well ahead of Britain in chemical and electrical manufactures. In the last thirty years of the 19th century Britain ceased to be the "workshop of the world" and became merely one of its three great industrial powers (Germany and the U.S.A. being the others) and, in some respects, the weakest of the three. It is easy to note examples of Britain's relative decline by looking at the tables.

Percentage Distribution of World Manufacturing Production

	1870	1913
U.S.A.	23.3	35.8
Germany	13.2	15.7
U.K.	31.8	14.0

Percentage Share of World Export Trade

	1876—1880	1913
U.K.	16.3	13.1
Central/Western Europe	31.9	33.4
U.S.A.	11.7	14.8

Coal Production: tons(m)

	1850	1860	1870	1880	1890	1900	1914
Germany	6	12	34	59	89	149	277
U.K.	57	81	112	149	184	228	292

Steel Production: tons(m)

	1870	1880	1890	1900	1910	1914
Germany	0.3	0.7	2.3	6.7	13.8	14.0
U.S.A.		1.3	4.3	10.0	26.0	32.0
U.K.	0.7	1.3	3.6	5.0	5.9	6.5

Why did this happen? It was not because the volume of British exports fell; it actually increased; nor was it because of a Balance of Payments problem (the difference between what a nation's economy earns and what it spends) for throughout the period the Balance of Payments was in surplus, mainly, it has been said, owing to the value of "invisibles" like shipping, banking, insurance and especially overseas investments.

One of the problems was that after 1870 the world was highly competitive. Once serious foreign competition was introduced, Britain's position had to be affected. A critical inquest began in Britain; for instance, E. E. Williams wrote:

> You will find that the material of some of your clothes was probably woven in Germany. Still more probable is it that some of your wife's garments are German importations . . . The toys and the dolls which your children maltreat in the nursery are made in Germany . . . Descend to your domestic depths, and you shall find your very drainpipes are German made.[1]

At home and abroad, Britain had to face the challenge of other European countries and of the U.S.A. Whatever market British goods entered, they were now faced with competition. And, because of

Britain's free trade policy, foreign goods could enter Britain without duty; yet other countries were erecting tariff barriers, with the result that British goods going into those countries had to pay duties, which of course made them more expensive and consequently less competitive.

Another reason for Britain's failure to remain supreme stems from the fact that she had industrialized before any other country. After the "early start", Britain's economic growth was dynamic. But there was a limit to the extent to which she could expand, and, naturally, her growth began to slow down. And this deceleration occurred just when Germany and the U.S.A. were "taking off".

Both government and industry in Britain were slow to appreciate the crucial significance of scientific and technical education. British educational institutions failed to turn out applied scientists in the numbers and of the quality turned out in Germany. German iron and steel companies frequently sent their foremen and managers on special scientific and technical courses. Just before 1914 Germany had 16,000 students in polytechnics; Britain had 4000. In 1901 Germany had 4500 trained industrial chemists; Britain had 1500. In 1907 G. D. Howard pointed out the road that he felt British businessmen should have followed:

> One of the most fundamental and important causes of the present prosperity of the German nation is the close relationship which exists in that country between science and practical affairs.

Many observers, concerned and worried by the fact that Britain was falling behind her major rivals, pointed accusing fingers at the complacency of her businessmen and industrialists. F. A. Mackenzie noted:

> If our workmen are slow, the masters are often enough right behind the times. In spite of all recent warnings there is solid conservatism about their methods which seems irremovable.[2]

This problem was summed up neatly by Veblen in 1915 when he remarked that the British economy was held back "... *by the restraining dead hand of past achievement.*"

A certain arrogance can be detected in the way British businessmen clung to the old methods that had been successful in the years of supremacy. *The Times* hit out at this attitude in 1912:

> [Businessmen] *often complain about unfair competition, but if any suggestion is made to them about improvements they excuse themselves in busy times by saying that they cannot afford to stop any part of their works for alterations, and in slack times they say they have no money to spend on new ideas.*

Reluctance to innovate was a serious flaw. Steelmakers moved over slowly to the so-called "direct" process which converted liquid pig iron to steel: only 28 per cent of British steel was made this way by 1913; Germany made 75 per cent of its steel by this method in 1900! The coal industry was reluctant to introduce coal-cutting machinery; shipbuilding, while it still enjoyed supremacy as producer of three-fifths of the world's tonnage in 1914, persisted with machinery that was growing obsolescent. Manufacturers, generally, were slow also to realize that increased efficiency and lower costs could have been achieved by standardized or mass production techniques. In this attitude they were reinforced largely by British market demands for a wide variety of different kinds of the same commodity to serve the various social groups. For instance, C. and J. Clark of Street offered hundreds of types of boots, shoes and slippers; Huntley and Palmer produced 400 varieties of biscuits. America had pointed the way to mass production with Ford's Model T on an assembly line by 1914. Only a few notable British manufacturers dared to copy American techniques; among them were Austin and Morris cars and Ransome's of Ipswich, the agricultural machine producer.

When Britain led the world, it was not necessary to send out armies of commercial travellers and customers were eager to buy. Neither was there a great need to pamper the foreign buyer by learning his language or by considering his every whim. Britain had the goods, and only Britain had them! But this approach did not win customers in the new competitive world. Towards the end of the 19th century the British Consul in Naples wrote:

> It is pitiable to see the British commercial traveller stumbling along with an interpreter, while his German counterpart is conversing fluently, and one is still more sorry for him when his patterns and samples are marked with British weights and measures.

Catalogues were usually in English, instead of in the language of the customers. Too few representatives were sent abroad. In 1899, for example, 28 British commercial travellers entered Switzerland, as against 3828 Germans and 1176 French. There was also an ignorance of local customs, and, worse, a failure to take account of the wishes of potential buyers.

During the Edwardian years the British economy did not stand still. At home there were important structural changes; considerable growth in multiple retailing in food, clothing, the sale of tobacco and newspapers, confectionery, soap, in entertainment, sport and journalism, insurance and public transport, gas lighting. The

THE UNCOMMERCIAL TRAVELLER.

Mr. Punch. "Now, Mr. Bull, wake up! You'll have to keep your eye on that chap. He's always at it, speaks their languages, and knows their money."
John Bull. "Pooh! My goods are better than his!"
Mr. Punch. "I daresay—but you've got to make them understand it!"

How Punch saw the trade position in 1901. Has it changed all that much?

names of firms engaged in these have become legendary: Lever
Brothers, Boots, Liptons, Home and Colonial, Marks and Spencer,
Rowntree, Cadbury, Harmsworth, Rothermere, Prudential. Consumer
durable goods also expanded in production in response mostly to
middle class demand—bicycles, stoves, sewing machines, pianos, and
even motor-cycles and cars. But the scale of this expansion should not
distract from the assessment that the Edwardian economy was not
completely healthy. While production had increased, as did exports, it
remained the case that the heavy staple industries on which the whole
economy depended showed signs of complacency, technological
inertia and a reluctance to innovate. This gave rise to concern. But
above all, relative to her major rivals, Germany and the U.S.A.,
Britain had lost her position of supremacy. Things were not as they
used to be.

---

[1]*Made in Germany* by E. E. Williams (HEINEMANN, 1896); [2]*The American
Invaders* by F. A. MacKenzie (1902)

8

Labour Unrest

*I*n 1909 a rising young economist, W. H. Beveridge, wrote:

Workmen today are men living on a quicksand, which at any moment may engulf individuals, which at uncertain intervals sinks for months or years below the sea surface altogether.[1]

Beveridge's "quicksand" was in fact "unemployment" which persisted at quite high levels throughout the Edwardian era and was one of the main reasons why in an age of so-called plenty so many people were in poverty. Yet both Conservative and Liberal governments paid a great deal of attention to the problem. 1905 saw the passage of the Unemployed Workmen's Bill; in 1909 Labour Exchanges were set up and in 1911 the National Insurance Act brought about a third of all adult male workers (some 2,250,000) into a state scheme of unemployment protection with a benefit of 7 shillings a week for a maximum of 15 weeks in any one year.

The Workers had themselves, throughout the years, expressed their concern about unemployment by trade union acitivity and, more publicly, through massive demonstrations. By 1908 so incensed were the workers at the rising tide of unemployment that trouble broke out in many of Britain's industrial centres. Demonstrations in London led to scuffles with the police and arrests were made. Windows were smashed in Manchester in protest against the Liberal Government's apparent dilatoriness about the problem. In Glasgow, workers from over forty trades took part in a massive anti-government demonstration at the end of June. Birmingham, too, had its share of trouble and even at Brighton the King's seaside residence was threatened by a crowd of angry unemployed. The infant Labour Party, at times quite half-heartedly according to the unemployed, took up the problem and its leaders, Ramsay MacDonald, George Lansbury and Arthur Henderson, put pressure on the Liberals for a "Right to Work" Bill. They wanted a register of the unemployed to be set up and conditions laid down whereby, if jobs could not be provided, state aid would be made available:

> *to provide maintenance should necessity exist for that person and for those depending on that person for the necessities of life.*

The Labour attempt came to nothing, but at least it did help to keep the seriousness of the problem in the ministers' minds.

Membership of the trade unions grew rapidly in this period: overall there was a doubling between 1900 and 1914, but more significant still was an increase of about two thirds between 1910 and 1913. The growing strength of the unions and the unemployment problem led the Government to investigate ways of preventing particularly the cyclical unemployment experienced by workers in certain industries, like building, shipbuilding and sawmilling.

Feeling its way with deliberate caution[2] was how one historian viewed the government's policy. But such a contentious issue demanded this approach. The Liberals thus produced a rather uncontroversial measure in the National Insurance Act of 1911, to follow upon the establishment of Labour Exchanges in 1909. The Act of 1911 was at least a start, and something of a cushion was provided for the workers worst affected by unemployment. The unions themselves were sceptical about a uniform government benefit scheme which cut across their own schemes. Lloyd George, however, sensibly decided not to weaken or destroy the existing friendly society and trade-union benefits, but to make the societies and unions agents for the operation of the state system. The result was that when the system started there was a rapid increase in membership of the societies and unions—sixty per cent in two years. The years after 1910 saw an improvement in the level of employment but while this problem lessened another appeared, equally serious, to replace it.

The early years of King Edward's reign had been, relatively, years of industrial peace, though they started badly as far as trade unionists were concerned. Legal rights was an issue in which the trade unions had become involved in the last years of the 19th century. But the decision of the House of Lords in 1901 over the Taff Vale dispute caused great anxiety among trade union leaders.

In August 1900 there had been a strike on the Taff Vale railway in South Wales. A signalman was alleged to have been victimized by his employers after he had led a movement for a pay rise; the men went on strike and were officially supported by their union, the Amalgamated Society of Railway Servants. Picketing was organized to prevent the company from employing black-leg labour, but the company's general manager decided to sue the union for financial compensation for his losses as a result of the picketing. The court awarded damages to the company, but the union took the matter to the Court of Appeal which reversed the first judgment. The employer then went to the House of Lords which restored the original decision. This was very important since it determined that the funds of a trade union were liable for damages inflicted by its officials. The Taff Vale Railway Company in fact was awarded about £30,000; the Union paid £23,000 and the rest was made up by legal costs. The details of the case were less important than the realization by the trade unions that such a decision weakened successful strike action in the future—union funds were liable for damages. The trade union leadership's hostility to the Taff Vale decision pushed them closer to the Labour Representation Committee and did much to give the foundation of the Labour Party union backing. In fact in 1903 a compulsory levy was made on the union membership to support Labour M.P.s. Three years later the Liberal Government restored the legal immunity of trade unions and allowed them to engage in peaceful picketing.

This sparked off serious industrial unrest, particularly among the better organized trade unions. For trade unionists their major grievance was a simple one—wages seemed to buy less and less. Price rises had taken place in many of the commodities that were basic to an average standard of living at a time when wage rates had become static. Between 1902 and 1909 the cost of living rose by four to five per cent. Between 1909 and 1913 it rose again by nearly nine per cent. Wages lagged behind. Unskilled workers were especially angry since their wages were very low, often below the poverty line. Another issue that added to trade union discontent in 1909 was, again, a decision of the House of Lords—this time it was the so-called "Osborne Judgment".

The case concerned W. V. Osborne, a member of the Liberal party, who was also secretary of the Walthamstow branch of the Union of Railway Servants. He decided to question the right of his union to take money from him as levy for a political party and brought an action before the courts to stop the union contributing to the upkeep of the Labour Party. The case was heard in the High Court in 1908 and Osborne's arguments were rejected. He then took it to the Court of Appeal which reversed the High Court decision. In December 1909 the House of Lords confirmed the opinion of the Court of Appeal. An injunction was therefore granted restraining the Railway Servants from raising a political levy for the Labour Party's funds. The decision hit the infant Labour Party hard, and, as a result, the party lent its weight to the unions' campaign for a reversal of the "Osborne judgment". Two year later in 1911 the money problem for Labour M.P.s was resolved by the Liberal Government's decision to pay M.P.s a salary. And in 1913 a Trade Union Act allowed political levies with conditions. To appease many middle-class Liberals who had become very anxious about the growth of trade union power shown by the great strikes of 1911 and 1912, the Government allowed union members, if they wanted, to contract out of paying the levy and union political funds were to be kept separate from other funds.

It was against this complex background of lagging wages, questions on the legal status of the unions and their political activities, that membership of the unions rose rapidly. Significant, too, was the fact that the biggest unions were keen to flex their muscles in the political arena. From 1910 the calm surface of the era was disturbed by constant labour unrest.

The autumn of 1910 saw strikes among miners in the Welsh valleys of Rhondda and Aberdare. In the spring of 1911 railwaymen on the North Eastern Railway struck for higher wages and better conditions. This was only one of many labour disputes in that year. Sailors, firemen, miners, dockers and others were involved in stoppages up and down the country. Street fights often marred the disputes: in Manchester, Liverpool and Wales police reinforcements were called in. Two men were shot dead in Liverpool and another two in Llanelly. It has been estimated that in 1911 there were 864 strikes and lock-outs involving about a million workers. Overall, more than ten million working days were lost by such disputes in that year alone.

From 26 February to 11 April 1912 miners were on strike, nationally, in support of a demand for a minimum wage of five shillings a shift for men and two shillings a shift for boys. Prime Minister Asquith brought the mine owners and workers together for a conference to settle the dispute, but it broke down. He took the unprecedented step of forcing a settlement by Act of Parliament. A Minimum Wages Bill was introduced on 19 March and received the Royal Assent on 29 March. This marked an important stage in the government of Britain: the State had, in fact, intervened directly in an industrial dispute—it was the first of many moves away from the traditional Liberal doctrine of *laissez-faire*. It did little to remove the grievances, and Labour unrest continued to dominate the last years before the war; in fact 1912 saw an unprecedented number of days lost through stoppages.

For a modern generation like ours, accustomed to organized trade unionism, it is hard to understand the worries and alarm with which ministers and people in the 1910–14 period regarded these industrial disputes. The able and astute Austen Chamberlain admitted:

we are living in a new world and the past gives us little guidance for the present.

The public and politicians' alarm was increased because they were baffled by what was happening, and, in such a situation, statements were made which we would today regard as outrageous and exaggerated. As early as 11 June 1900, *The Times* carried an article entitled "American Engineering Competition: the Labour Problem" and contained the following passage:

Militant trade unions have been the chief means of stopping the advance of British engineering industry, and in the interests of the men, as well as of the rest of the nation, their unreasonable and pernicious rule must be suppressed.

Fears were expressed about the marches of the unemployed and the danger to public order, especially in London where the East End unemployed usually routed themselves into the city's richer areas to collect money. But in 1903, the rise in unemployment to a figure of 5.6 per cent led the Home Secretary to increase police powers over these marches. By 1909 even greater fears existed among Government ministers and the general public about sectional discontents. The Suffragettes were, of course, in the forefront, but it seemed that Britain had entered a period of "industrial warfare". Organized Labour's demands for revolutionary changes were met by firm rebuffs from the Government and Liberal policy stayed much as it had been throughout its years of government from 1906.

Churchill had voiced the Liberal standpoint in 1906 at Glasgow:

the fortunes and interests of Liberalism and Labour are inseparably interwoven . . . That is why the Tory party hate us . . . The cause of the Liberal Party is the cause of the left-out millions.

Organized Labour was not satisfied with the Liberal Government's attempts to help the "left-out millions" and moved gradually to a stage of militancy which caused anxiety to authority. The coal strike in the Rhondda Valley in 1910–11, for instance, provoked the local authorities to appeal to the Home Secretary, Churchill, to send in troops to cope with the disorder. At Churchill's insistence the troops were strictly controlled so that they could not be regarded either by the miners as

More than 7000 unemployed from the East End of London marched to Hyde Park in November 1905, to demand work and condemn the dole.

strike-breakers or by the mine-owners as help to defeat the miners. It has rightly been claimed that:

> it is difficult to see what else a resolute Home Secretary could have done, given the situation in which such bitter industrial relations were allowed to develop.[3]

Yet in the rail strike of 1911 Churchill mobilized 50,000 troops supplied with twenty rounds of ammunition each and dispatched them to various strategic areas. Here Churchill went beyond his powers as Home Secretary because he ignored a regulation which forbade the use of troops unless they were specifically requested by the civil authority. It gave Labour's Ramsay MacDonald opportunity to challenge:

This is not a medieval state and it is not Russia; it is not even Germany . . . If the Home Secretary had just a bit more knowledge of how to handle men in these critical times, if he had a somewhat better instinct of what civil liberty does to men . . . we should have had much less difficulty during the last four or five days in facing and finally settling the problem.

Even the Liberal press, the *Daily News*, weighed in against the Home Secretary's

tendency to exaggerate a situation . . . the tendency that during the railway strike, dispatched the military hither and thither as though Armageddon was upon us.

But to numerous Edwardians and in Parliament, too, the unrest and worker militancy of the years 1910–14 was an ominous development. Syndicalist ideas from France and America had been taken up by a few thinkers, but contemporaries seem to have exaggerated their influence. A group of Welsh miners in 1912 issued a pamphlet called "The Miners' Next Step" which advocated drastic and militant action, including "irritation" strikes and go-slows. It aimed at the reduction of profits, in time, the elimination of capitalism, and the setting up of a Central Production Board which would decide, by statistical information that it collected, what the real needs of the people were. The Board would

issue its demands on the different departments of industry, leaving to the men themselves to determine under what conditions and how the work should be done.

The "Next Step" concluded that if such a scheme was adopted:

This would mean real democracy in real life, making for real manhood and womanhood. Any other form of democracy is a delusion and a snare.

Contemporaries were reluctant to admit that Britain was not a full democracy in the Edwardian era. Yet Mrs Pankhurst and the Suffragettes well publicized that females were outside the franchise; and such were the complexities of electoral qualifications that only sixty per cent of all adult males had the right to vote at parliamentary elections. Publications like "The Miners' Next Step" caused great concern among those who might have been more sympathetic to the workers' grievances. It also led many to believe that the wave of strikes was not just an attempt to improve wages and conditions of work but the beginning of a revolution. The days of deference were numbered.

The workers now knew what they wanted—the growth of the press had seen to that as H. G. Wells wrote in the *Daily Mail* of 1912 in an article entitled "What the Worker Wants":

The working man of today reads, talks, has general ideas and a sense of the world; he is far nearer to the ruler of today in knowledge and intellectual range than he is to the working man of fifty years ago . . . The old workman might and did quarrel very vigorously with his specific employer, but he never set out to arraign all employers.[4]

Politicians, like Churchill, recognized also that they had new ambitions:

They demand time to look about them, time to see their homes by daylight, to see their children, time to think and read and cultivate their gardens— time, in short, to live.

It was, with this in mind, that the Liberals pressed on with their social legislation. As Lloyd George declared:

I can see the Old Age Pensions Act and the National Insurance Act and many another Act in their trail, descending like breezes from the hills of my native land, sweeping into the mist-laden valleys, and clearing the gloom away, until the rays of God's sun have pierced the narrowest window.

This was a large claim to make. The workers of the Edwardian era remained discontented. In fewer than 25 per cent of the disputes, according to the figures of the Board of Trade, were workers' wage claims settled. In most cases the workers returned to work without gaining their target completely. There was greater pressure for larger, more organized unions over a whole industry so that more pressure could be exerted over employers; but only the railwaymen succeeded with this in the years before the war. Even more dangerous potentially for industrial peace was the idea in 1913 of the "Triple Alliance" of miners, transport workers and railwaymen, which could bring the country to a standstill at any time by calling a general strike.

The industrial strife of late Edwardian Britain was not swept away by Liberal legislation or negotiation; the workers' "gloom" was merely replaced by another—the gloom of the war that broke out in August 1914.

---

[1]*Unemployment* by W. H. Beveridge (LONGMANS, 1909); [2]*Edwardian England* by D. Read (HARRAP, 1972); [3]"Churchill and the Trade Unions" by G. Isaacs, in *Churchill by his Contemporaries* by C. Eade (ed.) (HUTCHINSON, 1953); [4]*What the Worker Wants* by H. G. Wells (HODDER & STOUGHTON, 1912)

Further Sources

Documentary Sources

Documents from Edwardian England   ed. D. Read   (HARRAP, 1973)
The Liberals and the Welfare State   R. D. H. Seaman (ARNOLD, 1968)

Reference

Edwardian England 1901–1914   ed. S. Nowell-Smith   (OXFORD, 1964)
The Twentieth Century Mind 1: 1900–1918   ed. C. B. Cox & A. E. Dyson
(OXFORD, 1972)

General Reading

Social History of Edwardian Britain   J. Bishop   (ANGUS & ROBERTSON, 1977)
Edwardian England   D. Read   (HARRAP, 1972)
Edward VII   C. Hibbert   (ALLEN LANE, 1976)
The Life and Times of Edward VII   K. Middlemas   (WEIDENFELD & NICOLSON, 1972)
The Edwardians   P. Thompson   (WEIDENFELD & NICOLSON, 1975)
Life in Edwardian England   R. Cecil   (BATSFORD, 1969)
The Edwardians   J. B. Priestley   (HEINEMANN, 1970)
The Ragged Trousered Philanthropists   R. Tressell   (LAWRENCE & WISHART, 1965)
The Militant Suffragettes   A. Raeburn   (MICHAEL JOSEPH, 1973)

Fiction

The Edwardians   V. Sackville-West   (HOGARTH, 1930)
The Dubliners   J. Joyce   (PENGUIN, 1914)

Lark Rise to Candleford F. Thompson (OXFORD, 1945; PENGUIN)
Tono-Bungay H. G. Wells (MACMILLAN, 1905)
Kipps H. G. Wells (MACMILLAN, 1905)
Ann Veronica H. G. Wells (UNWIN, 1909)
The Man of Property J. Galsworthy (PENGUIN)
Howard's End E. M. Forster (PENGUIN)

and some for the ever young

The Wind in the Willows K. Grahame (METHUEN, 1908)
Peter Pan J. M. Barrie (PENGUIN)
Kim R. Kipling (MACMILLAN; PAN)

Journals

The Illustrated London News
Punch

Assignments

1. "*Pauperism is a token of the inferior quality which belongs to an inferior stock. The hereditary nature of this incapacity may lighten the moral reproach against the loafer and the vagrant, but it emphasises the necessity of protecting the community against them, and, in particular, of protecting it against the perpetuation of the degenerate stocks which they represent.*"

(*Control of the Idle Poor* by N. Pearson, 1911)

a. What is meant by "*moral reproach*"?

b. How can Rowntree's analysis of the causes of poverty be used to refute Pearson's first sentence "*Pauperism . . . stock*"?

c. What provisions existed in the Edwardian era for "*protecting the community against them*" and how successful were these?

d. How did the measures of the Liberals deal with the problem of the "*perpetuation of the degenerate stocks*"?

2. Asquith drew up a list of potential peers as part of his strategy to overcome the resistance of the Lords to the People's Budget and the Parliament Bill. It included the following:

The Right Hon. Sir George O. Trevelyan; H. J. Tennant M.P.; Sir William H. Lever; Sir H. Harmsworth; The Hon. Bertrand Russell; W. S. Haldane; Frank Lloyd; Joseph Rowntree; Gilbert Murray; Thomas Hardy; Frank Debenham; J. M. Barrie; Sir Thomas Lipton.

Find out as much as you can about each of them and indicate why they were worthy of elevation to the Edwardian House of Lords.

MUNICIPAL WARDS		1 APARTMENTS		2 APARTMENTS		3 APARTMENTS	
		No.	Inhabi-tants	No.	Inhabi-tants	No.	Inhabi-tants
1	Dalmarnock	4,036	13,701	5,873	31,776	788	4,823
2	Calton	2,360	7,059	3,503	17,424	1,283	7,193
3	Mile-End	3,343	11,285	5,477	29,003	711	4,624
4	Whitevale	1,644	5,407	3,517	17,185	1,305	7,471
5	Dennistoun	721	2,032	3,644	15,080	2,631	12,434
6	Springburn	2,606	9,073	5,500	28,048	939	5,813
7	Cowlairs	1,328	4,397	3,627	17,991	1,089	6,216
8	Townhead	1,569	4,740	4,119	20,251	1,354	7,690
9	Blackfriars	1,073	3,220	1,930	9,484	761	4,489
10	Exchange	49	126	87	379	80	406
11	Blythswood	22	4	73	253	75	327
12	Broomielaw	205	581	611	2,989	301	1,715
13	Anderston	1,183	3,608	3,160	14,820	1,193	6,816
14	Sandyford	750	2,323	1,889	9,087	1,236	6,475
15	Park	105	249	632	2,517	896	4,031
16	Cowcaddens	1,788	5,202	3,420	17,340	1,362	7,333
17	Woodside	1,691	4,944	4,836	22,438	1,647	8,630
18	Hutchesontown	2,876	9,313	5,068	26,155	620	4,002
19	Gorbals	1,076	3,156	2,761	12,741	2,102	11,480
20	Kingston	1,100	3,494	2,884	13,596	2,129	11,286
21	Govanhill	1,054	3,449	4,352	19,539	1,690	8,934
22	Langside	62	195	2,036	7,322	3,645	14,367
23	Pollokshields	45	146	263	1,099	213	888
24	Kelvinside	15	34	175	775	964	3,387
25	Maryhill	1,231	4,024	4,659	22,345	1,436	7,370
26	Kinning Park	810	2,842	1,440	7,704	325	1,883
	CITY	32,742	104,641	75,536	367,341	30,775	160,083

according to the size of their houses (exclusive of institutions),
empty houses in each municipal ward.

4 APARTMENTS		5 APARTMENTS AND UPWARDS		TOTAL INHABITED HOUSES	TOTAL INHABITANTS	WINDOWED ROOMS	EMPTY HOUSES
No.	Inhabitants	No.	Inhabitants				
76	492	47	369	10,820	51,161	18,769	1,564
256	1,515	241	1,949	7,643	35,140	15,901	885
80	483	38	257	9,649	45,652	17,007	1,321
219	1,361	72	507	6,757	31,931	13,840	848
780	4,066	477	2,602	8,253	36,214	22,233	877
176	961	173	918	9,394	44,813	18,247	1,524
82	465	58	375	6,184	29,444	12,523	990
404	2,563	204	1,425	7,650	36,469	16,919	866
194	1,242	139	1,518	4,097	19,953	9,134	537
57	294	45	467	318	1,672	1,397	40
137	637	208	1,537	515	2,795	3,031	64
131	881	44	586	1,292	6,752	3,391	236
257	1,464	149	1,015	5,942	27,723	13,070	639
405	2,159	685	3,552	4,965	23,596	14,523	507
1,445	6,520	1,634	8,990	4,712	22,307	22,561	499
393	2,283	244	1,740	7,207	33,898	15,894	1,272
491	2,585	467	2,601	9,132	41,198	21,496	1,074
45	295	21	166	8,630	39,931	15,193	926
537	3,331	360	2,484	6,836	33,192	17,197	833
545	3,144	170	1,156	6,828	32,676	16,399	840
405	2,213	169	947	7,670	35,082	17,391	980
1,774	7,649	1,844	9,355	9,361	38,888	34,312	941
757	3,017	2,336	11,974	3,614	17,124	21,969	387
680	2,615	2,607	12,992	4,441	19,803	26,555	561
465	2,045	723	3,575	8,514	39,359	21,771	1,456
26	158	39	254	2,640	12,841	4,989	230
10,817	54,238	13,194	73,311	163,064	759,614	415,802	20,897

3. The *Glasgow Herald* of Tuesday 10 March 191₄ carried these headlines:

MRS PANKHURST ARRESTED IN GLASGOW
FIGHT IN ST. ANDREW'S HALL
POLICE STORM THE PLATFORM
SEVERAL PERSONS INJURED

Find out how your local newspaper reported the Suffragettes, or write a letter expressing your opinion of Sir Almroth Wright's views on women.

4. Study the table on pages 80–81, then answer these questions.

a. Which percentage of the population of Glasgow lived in: one apartment; two apartments; two or less apartments?

b. How far can these figures reveal or conceal over-crowding (according to the Registrar General's criterion)?

c. Why are windowed rooms specially mentioned?

d. Deduce why Exchange and Blythswood (both city centre wards) have so few inhabitants?

e. Mile-End is in the city's East End. What conclusions can be drawn about housing conditions there?

f. Kelvinside and Maryhill are adjacent wards in the West End. Calculate the average number of inhabitants per house type for both wards and suggest, by using the figures obtained, which ward was better to live in. Which ward would you label middle class and which working class?